As part of the *PocketArchitecture* Series, this volume focuses on inclusive design and its allied fields – ergonomics, accessibility, and participatory design. This book aims for the direct application of inclusive design concepts and technical information into architectural and interior design practices, construction, facilities management, and property development. A central goal is to illustrate the aesthetic, experiential, qualitative, and economic consequences of design decisions and methods. The book is intended to be a "first-source" reference – at the desk or in the field – for design professionals, contractors and builders, developers, and building owners.

Jordana L. Maisel is Director of Research Activities at the Center for Inclusive Design and Environmental Access and an Assistant Research Professor in the School of Architecture and Urban and Regional Planning at the University at Buffalo, USA. Her primary research focuses on advancing universal design and investigating the relationship between health outcomes and the built environment. Maisel is co-author of *Universal Design: Creating Inclusive Environments* (2012) and co-editor of *Accessible Public Transportation: Designing Service for Riders with Disabilities* (Routledge, 2017). She holds a PhD in Industrial and Systems Engineering and a Master of Urban Planning degree.

Edward Steinfeld is a Distinguished SUNY Professor of Architecture at the University at Buffalo, USA. He is a registered architect, with special interests in universal design, accessibility, and design for the life span. Steinfeld founded and still directs the Center for Inclusive Design and Environmental Access. He has been the Principal Investigator for four cycles of a federally funded center of excellence on universal design and the built environment and co-directs another on accessible public transportation. He received his Masters and Doctorate in Architecture at the University of Michigan, USA.

Megan Basnak is an Architectural Design and Research Associate at the Center for Inclusive Design and Environmental Access, where her research interests include investigating architectural practice that aids underserved populations, the impact of universal design on different user groups, and universal design education in the United States and abroad. She has also co-authored several publications including a book chapter in *Diversity and Design: Understanding Hidden Consequences* (Routledge, 2015) and has presented at several conferences in the United States and internationally. She holds a Master of Architecture degree.

Korydon Smith is a Professor in the School of Architecture and Planning at the University at Buffalo, USA, where he conducts research on design for diversity, health, and social justice. Smith is the author/editor of numerous books, including co-editorship of *Diversity and Design: Understanding Hidden Consequences* (Routledge, 2015) and editor of *Introducing Architectural Theory: Debating a Discipline* (Routledge, 2012). Smith holds an EdD in Higher Education Leadership as well as a professional Master of Architecture degree.

M. Beth Tauke is an Associate Professor in the Department of Architecture at the University at Buffalo, USA, where she teaches courses on design, diversity, and the human body/architecture relationship. Her research focuses on design education and inclusive design, especially the empowerment of underrepresented groups through design. She is co-editor of *Universal Design: New York* (NYC Mayor's Office, 2001) and *Diversity and Design: Understanding Hidden Consequences* (Routledge, 2015).

PocketArchitecture: Technical Design Series

Series Editor: Ryan E. Smith

Building Information Modeling
Karen M. Kensek

Life Cycle Assessment
Kathrina Simonen

Daylighting and Integrated Lighting Design
Christopher Meek and Kevin Van Den Wymelenberg

Architectural Acoustics
Ana M. Jaramillo and Chris Steel

The Hierarchy of Energy in Architecture
Ravi Srinivasan and Kiel Moe

Design Management
Stephen Emmitt

Inclusive Design
*Jordana L. Maisel, Edward Steinfeld, Megan Basnak,
Korydon Smith, and M. Beth Tauke*

PocketArchitecture:
Technical Design Series

Inclusive Design
Implementation and Evaluation

Jordana L. Maisel, Edward Steinfeld, Megan Basnak,
Korydon Smith, and M. Beth Tauke

Routledge
Taylor & Francis Group

LONDON AND NEW YORK

First published 2018
by Routledge
2 Park Square, Milton Park, Abingdon, Oxon OX14 4RN

and by Routledge
711 Third Avenue, New York, NY 10017

Routledge is an imprint of the Taylor & Francis Group, an informa business

© 2018 Jordana L. Maisel, Edward Steinfeld, Megan Basnak,
Korydon Smith, and M. Beth Tauke

British Library Cataloguing-in-Publication Data
A catalogue record for this book is available from the British Library

Library of Congress Cataloging-in-Publication Data
Names: Maisel, Jordana, author. | Steinfeld, Edward, author. |
    Basnak, Megan, author. | Smith, Korydon H., 1977– author. |
    Tauke, Beth, author.
Title: Inclusive design : implementation and evaluation / Jordana L.
    Maisel, Edward Steinfeld, Megan Basnak, Korydon Smith, and
    M. Beth Tauke.
Description: New York : Routledge, 2017. | Series:
    PocketArchitecture : technical design series | Includes
    bibliographical references and index.
Identifiers: LCCN 2017023072 | ISBN 9781138890343 (hb :
    alk. paper) | ISBN 9781138890350 (pb : alk. paper) | ISBN
    9781315712437 (ebook)
Subjects: LCSH: Architectural design—Methodology. | Design—
    Methodology. | Architectural practice.
Classification: LCC NA2750 .M185 2017 | DDC 729—dc23
LC record available at https://lccn.loc.gov/2017023072

ISBN: 978-1-138-89034-3 (hbk)
ISBN: 978-1-138-89035-0 (pbk)
ISBN: 978-1-315-71243-7 (ebk)

Typeset in Goudy and Univers
by Apex CoVantage, LLC
Printed in Canada

Contents

List of figures   *viii*

Series editor's preface   *x*

Authors' preface: practicing inclusive design   *xii*

An introduction to inclusive design   **1**

Chapter 1 Pre-design   **13**

Chapter 2 Design   **46**

Chapter 3 Construction   **97**

Chapter 4 Occupancy   **125**

Index   *137*

Figures

1.1	Normal distribution bell curve	18
1.2	Urban transect	27
1.3	Non-pedestrian friendly street design	29
1.4	McDonald's with turquoise arches in Sedona, Arizona	30
2.1	Pavers providing a track for wheeled mobility devices	48
2.2	Walkway system connecting two levels on the J. Paul Getty Museum Campus in Los Angeles, California	50
2.3	Evacuation of nursing home patients amid Hurricane Katrina in New Orleans, Louisiana	51
2.4	Options for vertical movement within a building	54
2.5	Tactile floor leading to information desk	54
2.6	Wayfinding in Stuttgart City Library by Yi Architects	55
2.7	Wayfinding system in medical office	57
2.8	LED lighting in retail setting	59
2.9	General, ambient, and task lighting in kitchen	60
2.10	Top-lighting strategies	63
2.11	Raised walkway system at Naples Botanical Garden, Naples, Florida	67
2.12	Protected walkway at Naples Botanical Garden in Naples, Florida	67
2.13	Boardwalk at Cape Cod National Seashore in Provincetown, Massachusetts	69
2.14	Cues at transitional moments on stairs in the House of Disabled People's Organisations in Taastrup, Denmark	70
2.15	Ramp to entrance of home	72
2.16	Sloping residential entry path in home show house by Heartland Homes	73

2.17	Raised dishwasher in home show house by Heartland Homes	75
2.18	Inclusive residential kitchen	76
2.19	Carpet on glass floor and stairway in retail store	81
2.20	Sociopetal seating arrangement in university residence hall	84
2.21	Suspended acoustic treatment in university presentation space	85
2.22	Talking map at the Perkins School for the Blind by Touch Graphics Inc. and the University at Buffalo IDeA Center	86
2.23	Kitchen in the LIFEhouse, a universally designed home developed by New American Homes in Antioch, Illinois	93
3.1	Dual-height water fountains with bottle filler	99
3.2	Renovated library with dual ramps	101
3.3	Foundation detail to achieve a zero-step entry using a reverse brick ledge	113
3.4	Ramped sill detail to eliminate high threshold	114
3.5	Adaptable bathroom vanity cabinet with removable base in Wounded Warrior home by Clark Realty Capital LLC	117
4.1	Trash can placement resulting in unintended obstacles to movement	128
4.2	Greiner Hall, University at Buffalo, New York	131

Series editor's preface

Although architects and building professionals come in to contact with, specify, design, and build technical practices every day, they actually know relatively little about them. They are "abstract systems" construed and constructed upon industry norms passed through generations of professionals. Most of them are correct, but many, when disassociated with their cultural underpinnings of building vernacular and, more important, their scientific basis and practice contexts, present challenges that cause buildings to not perform as intended or, worse, lead to physical, economic, or social catastrophe.

PocketArchitecture: Technical Design Series fills this void. The series comprises succinct, easy to use, topic-based volumes that collate in one place unbiased, need-to-know technical information about specific subject areas by expert authors. This series demystifies technical design criteria and solutions. It presents information without overladen theory or anecdotal information. PocketArchitecture is on point.

As the name would suggest, the volumes in this series are pocket sized and collectively serve as a knowledge base on technical subjects in architecture, creating a value-added information base for building novices and masters alike. In addition to architects, engineers, and contractors who deliver building projects, the series is appropriate for students and academics interested in accessible information on technical information as it relates to building design and construction.

Despite their size, the series volumes are highly illustrated. Furthermore, the volumes use easily accessible language to succinctly explain the fundamental concepts and then apply these basic ideas to cases of common issues encountered in the built environment. PocketArchitecture is essential, accessible, and authoritative. This makes it important reading for architectural technologists, architects, building surveyors, building commissioners, building engineers, other construction professionals, even owners and clients.

This volume, *Inclusive Design: Implementation and Evaluation*, is written by the following team of researchers from the Center for Inclusive Design and Environmental Access (IDeA Center), University at Buffalo: Jordana L. Maisel, Edward Steinfeld, Megan Basnak, Korydon Smith, and M. Beth Tauke. Since 1984, the IDeA Center has been practicing human-centered design through research, service, and teaching to both academic and professional audiences. As experts, the authors have created a need-to-know volume for any designer of the built environment seeking to be inclusive and implement universal design principles into practice. The volume encourages architects to focus on the process or practice of inclusive design in addition to the end product. Further, inclusive design as presented herein is a means for creative design thinking, giving rise to a more holistic design solution that can meet not only the needs of an immediate client, but also society more broadly with varying abilities. As part of the PocketArchitecture Series, the book includes both fundamental principles and implementation strategies. It is appropriate for the novice and expert practitioner, as its content is fresh and well considered in the field of texts on inclusive design.

Ryan E. Smith,
Senior Editor
Design Management:
PocketArchitecture series

Authors' preface:
practicing inclusive design

Twenty years ago, most architects and construction professionals had not heard of inclusive design or any of its synonyms: universal design, design-for-all, life span design, or human-centered design. Today, inclusive design is known worldwide for fostering environments, products, communications, systems, and policies that work for more people. The premise is that, if a design works across the full range of human abilities, it will be more functional, satisfying, and marketable. The recent popularity of this movement has been driven, in large part, by the aging of the world population and renewed global interests in social equity.

Inclusive processes "that enable and empower a diverse population by improving human performance, health and wellness, and social participation" have been around since the mid-twentieth century. With roots in the Civil Rights and Disability Rights movements of the United States, United Kingdom, and elsewhere, inclusive design is socially focused and grounded in democratic values of non-discrimination, equal opportunity, and personal empowerment.[1]

This abbreviated history of inclusive design in the built environment includes key components of its evolution:

1950s

"Barrier-free" designers began the early work of removing obstacles in the built environment for people with physical disabilities, especially in Europe, Japan, and the United States, in response to the aftermath of World War II, that is, severely injured veterans returning home to war-torn cities, and social policies that encouraged people with disabilities to move from institutional settings back into their communities.

1960s

Social empowerment movements (feminism, civil rights, etc.) brought new attention to equal rights and social justice. People on the margins of society (including those with disabilities) rallied for change and influenced designers and policy makers. In the United Kingdom, architect Selwyn Goldsmith wrote the groundbreaking *Designing for the Disabled* (1963), an indispensable architectural access guide for built environment professionals throughout the world. In the United States, new standards and policies were established, such as *American Standard Specifications for Making Buildings and Facilities Accessible to, and Usable by, the Physically Handicapped* (1961), which became the basis for subsequent architectural access codes. The Architectural Barriers Act (1968) required accessibility in all U.S. federally owned or leased buildings, including restrooms.

1970s

Fueled by the Civil Rights and Women's Rights movements, the Disability Rights movement spread throughout Europe and North America. Advocates argued against the *medical model* of disability, in which impairments are considered primarily as medical problems with medical solutions, and toward the *social model*, in which disability is defined by the relationships between people and their built and social environments. Disconnects can be caused by inadequate design, ineffectual services and environments, and/or cultural stereotypes. Activists demanded "accessible design," which moved away from adaptive solutions and toward normalization and integration. Design became part of the social equity equation.

1980s

The concepts of "barrier-free" and "accessible" design evolved into a new concept, coined "universal design" in 1983 by architect Ron Mace, who claimed that design that works for those who are disabled also works better for the entire population. Mace convened a working group of architects, product designers, engineers, and environmental design researchers who developed the Seven Principles of Universal Design (UD), thus, formalizing the UD movement. Three centers were founded in the United States: the Institute for Human Centered Design in Boston, formerly Adaptive Environments (1978), the Center for Inclusive Design and Environmental Access (IDeA) at the University at Buffalo – State University of New York, formerly The Adaptive Environments Laboratory (1984), and the Center for Universal Design at North Carolina State University, formerly the Center for Accessible Housing (1989). These centers developed agendas for research, teaching, and practice and promoted universal design concepts to government entities. In 1988, the Council for Interior Design Accreditation in the United States required that students in accredited programs demonstrate an understanding of accommodations for special populations, including people with disabilities, older adults, and children in both residential and non-residential environments. During this same decade, the United Nations proclaimed 1983 to 1992 to be the Decade of Disabled Persons and encouraged global policies offering their equal rights.

1990s

Influenced by groundbreaking legislation, the concept of universal design spread. The 1990 Americans with Disabilities Act (ADA) outlawed discrimination based on mental and/or physical disabilities and prodded accessibility requirements for public buildings. The 1995 Disability Discrimination Act in the United Kingdom prohibited discrimination against people with disabilities in relation to employment, the provision of goods and services, education, and transportation. Legislation was also passed in other countries throughout the world. Many governments recognized that changes in the built environment were beneficial for the whole population. In response, additional organizations and centers were established in Europe, including Design for All Europe (1993) and the Helen Hamlyn Centre for Design (1999), where director Roger Coleman used the term "inclusive design." During this time, the National Endowment for the Arts also supported the Universal Design Education Project directed by Elaine Ostroff, and university courses in universal design were offered in design programs across the United States and United Kingdom.

2000s

At the start of the next millennium, the concept of universal design went global and widened its focus from design for disabilities to the improvement of people's lives across a range of social groups and human needs. Conferences were hosted throughout the world, including the International Association for Universal Design Conference and the Royal College of Art's Include, both held biannually. In 2001, the World Health Organization (WHO) redefined disability through the International Classification of Functioning, Disability and Health and emphasized functional status over diagnoses. Disability was described as a contextual variable, intersecting with social and economic status. Inclusive design was cited as a strategy for enhancing people's daily experiences and lifelong attainment. In addition, in 2006, the United Nations General Assembly adopted the Convention on the Rights of People with Disabilities. During this decade, a number of African countries passed legislation to improve rights for people with disabilities, including South Africa (2000), Kenya (2003), and Tunisia (2005). In 2009, the Norwegian government published an action plan (via the Soria Moria Declaration), with a goal to have the country universally designed by 2025. Researchers, including Edward Steinfeld, director of the IDeA Center, developed programs that provided the evidence base necessary to help designers develop solid solutions to expand use of the built environment and convince practitioners in the building and manufacturing industries that inclusive design was good business practice. The first graduate program focusing on inclusive design (Master of Architecture with a specialization in inclusive design) was established at the University at Buffalo in 2008.

2010s

Inclusive design impacts on the marketplace became evident at international builders' shows, where manufacturers promoted universally designed building products, especially for entrances, offices, kitchens, and bathrooms. Concomitantly, inclusive design expanded to global issues of social justice, particularly in developing countries. In 2015, leaders at the General Assembly of the United Nations made several commitments (which overlap inclusive design principles) to improve the lives of disenfranchised populations throughout the world, including people with disabilities. Universal design developed into an established field of study and was incorporated into many industrial design, interior design, and architecture curricula. In 2016, an IDeA Center team launched *innovative solutions for Universal Design (isUD)*, evidence-based universal design solutions for the built environment, which were funded by the National Institute on Disability, Independent Living, and Rehabilitation Research (NIDILRR). The United Nations Sustainable Development Goals, adopted in 2015, set aggressive, global targets to be achieved by 2030 in the sectors of health, education, water, sanitation, energy, and nutrition. Underpinning all areas is an emphasis on equality, cross-sector partnerships, and sustainability, key tenets of inclusive design.

Going Forward

Inclusive design has continued to gain momentum for a number of reasons:

- *Demographics are changing.* Over the next twenty years, the older population will increase by more than 50% in many developed countries. The WHO estimates that over 1 billion people, or 15% of the world's population, currently have some form of disability. As demographics change, this number will dramatically increase. Inclusively designed products, systems, and environments that empower this growing population will be in greater demand in the coming years.
- *Social sustainability is a natural part of the environmental sustainability movement and contemporary business practices.* "Social sustainability is focused on the development of programs and processes [and products] that promote social interaction and cultural enrichment. It emphasizes protecting the vulnerable, respecting social diversity, and ensuring that we all put priority on social capital. Social sustainability is related to how we make choices that affect other humans in our 'global community'." Inclusive design is a facet of social sustainability.[2]
- *Mass customization is making it easier to develop inclusively designed solutions.* Mass customization is the application of flexible computer-aided manufacturing systems to produce customized goods and services.

Through this process, products that were once standardized are now able to change to meet the needs of individuals at the same low unit costs of mass production. This approach to manufacturing makes inclusive design more possible and affordable.

- *Digital technologies are augmenting or eliminating static solutions to dynamic conditions.* Many previously fixed products and systems are now active. For example, Global Positioning Systems (GPS) augment environmental signage and provide individual navigation and information that is specific to each user's needs. Dynamic and personalized products and systems add a critical layer of usability for everyone.

- *World economies are changing.* The International Monetary Fund World Economic Outlook states that although downside risks have diminished overall, there is increased financial volatility in emerging market economies, and increases in the cost of capital will likely dampen investment and weigh on growth. This forecast moves attention toward smart conservation – ways to save money that maintain or improve standards of living. As a result, businesses and governments are looking at processes and approaches that change patterns of waste. Inclusive design, then, becomes part of the solution. For example, the cost of assisted living and nursing facility care is expensive, both for national health providers and individuals/families. Vast amounts of money will be saved if people can stay in their houses or apartments longer because they are inclusively designed.[3]

- *Attitudes about consumption are changing.* The concepts of "planned obsolescence" and "consumer waste" so prevalent in the latter part of the twentieth century are giving way to more prudent and conscientious notions of consumption. Rising energy costs and the slowdown in the world economy have encouraged consumers to rethink their purchasing patterns. Quality over quantity is making a comeback. Inclusively designed features save money in the long run and elevate the quality of living for all.

The promise of inclusive design in the built environment has yet to be fully realized, but has made great strides in the past several decades. It has become a foundational element of policy makers, planners, business professionals, manufacturers, design practitioners, design educators, researchers, and government officials. In the end, practicing inclusive design provides access to many worlds – for people who might be physically, cognitively, economically, culturally, or technologically excluded – and offers greater social participation, satisfaction, and achievement.

Notes

1 Steinfeld, Edward, and Jordana L. Maisel. *Universal Design: Creating Inclusive Environments*. Hoboken, NJ: John Wiley & Sons, 2012; and Tauke, Beth. "Universal Design – The Time Is Now." In www.uigarden.net/english/universal-design-the-time-is-now, ed. by C. Li. Apogee, Usability in Asia, 2008.
2 Vavik, Tom, and Martina Maria Keitsch. "Exploring Relationships Between Universal Design and Social Sustainable Development: Some Methodological Aspects to the Debate on the Sciences of Sustainability." *Sustainable Development* 18.5 (2010): 295–305.
3 International Monetary Fund. "World Economic Outlook: Legacies, Clouds, Uncertainties, 2014." www.imf.org/external/pubs/ft/weo/2014/02/pdf/text.pdf (accessed March 10, 2017).

An introduction to inclusive design

There is an architectural adage that "eccentric clients make for eccentric buildings." (A similar proverb may be made about eccentric architects.) Embedded in the axiom are several assumptions: that, for example, curious personas desire strange surroundings, or that architects play only a secondary, facilitative role in the design of buildings. The adage also assumes a linear relationship between clients and buildings, where external influences – other stakeholders, structural limitations, legal restrictions, budgetary constraints, and so forth – are removed from the project such that only the wishes of the client remain. While there are examples of eccentric clients, architects, and buildings (presumably several come to the minds of the readers of this book), the vast majority of architectural projects involve a multitude of influences and decision makers. Even for a modest single-family dwelling, an architect mediates an ongoing and evolving discussion that includes the client, the client's family, local governments, consultants, construction managers, and tradespeople – even neighbors.

One aim of this book, therefore, is to provide practical guidance on navigating the conversations that occur with a multitude of stakeholders for each phase of a project – from pre-design, to design, to construction, and into post-occupancy. Equally important is identifying the stakeholders whose voices are unheard or underheard, gaining their feedback, and coalescing it in order to improve the quality and success of an architectural project.

A second aim is to provide practical tips for incorporating inclusive design methods, principles, and strategies into the four project phases listed previously. Unlike meeting accessibility codes, which often occurs as a "review" in the middle phases of design, the inclusive design approach emerges at the very beginning of a project, runs throughout the duration of design and construction, and contributes to post-occupancy evaluations and architectural research.

What is inclusive design? Why is it important?

Buildings are complicated and expensive. Done well, buildings inspire and safeguard. Done poorly, they frustrate and injure. Done well, buildings gain in value. Done poorly, they devalue. The goal here is to provide practical methods and strategies for improving the likelihood of long-term building success in meeting (or exceeding) client and occupant contentment.

Inclusive design is a holistic approach to the process of developing and creating products, buildings, landscapes, systems, and cities. Designing for human diversity – in regards to age, gender, race, religion, personality, and other factors – is central, particularly in addressing the wide spectrum of physical, sensory, and cognitive abilities that comprise society. Global migration, longer life spans, trends in disease and disability, and general demographic diversification of societies prompt the need for alternative design processes and strategies. The functions, activities, and users of buildings have also expanded, as evidenced in the rise in the number of children's museums, intergenerational residences, recreational facilities, and high-tech research centers. In short, buildings serve more diverse occupants than ever before.

Nevertheless, social diversity is not isolated; it is intertwined with other factors of architectural design, such as economics, aesthetics, and sustainability. Today's building owners – tech savvy, health conscious, and economically astute – are more aware of how buildings impact their own and their stakeholders' well-being, productivity, and happiness, and are willing to advocate for what they think is best. Today's building occupants are equally perceptive. From façade design, to building layout, to lighting and acoustics, to furniture selection: building design affects client and user perceptions, performance, and satisfaction; and they know it. These elements, in turn, influence the value of a building and the profitability of the business that occupies it, the desirability of a residence and the tenure of its tenants, the longevity of a school or museum, and the future visitors it draws.

The principles, goals, and processes of inclusive design

The aim of inclusive design is frequently described in terms of outcomes, for example, a product or building being functional for and usable by the greatest percentage of the population possible. Through this thinking, designers (and their clients) sought incremental improvements to the objects and spaces they designed in order to capture a larger and larger user group. In part, what emerged was a generation of designers that searched for and strived to understand as many unique physiological, biological, and developmental "conditions" as possible. While seeking out less common and highly varied examples of human ability did stretch designers' thinking and their work into new realms, the early phases of inclusive design remained idiosyncratic, stemming simply from the unique cases each designer chose to consider. A common framework was needed.

This charge led to the creation of the Seven Principles of Universal Design, developed in 1997 by a group of experts convened through the Center for Universal Design at North Carolina State University. "Equitable Use," or the principle of non-segregating, non-stigmatizing design, was the foundational principle. Other principles focused on flexibility, intuitiveness, perceptibility, tolerance for error, amount of effort required, and space for maneuvering and use. While the Principles provided a common framework for research and practice, and gained momentum over the subsequent two decades, three shortcomings became clear. First, the Principles emphasized the built environment, but did not include allied domains, such as the design of systems and services (e.g., communications systems or customer service), which modulate the performance of the built environment. Second, the Principles were drafted from a high-income, Western context, and did not fully consider the nuances and limitations of design in rural, low-resource, or global contexts. Third, the Principles emphasized the human-environment interface as objective and universal, but did not fully integrate the role of sociocultural factors.

Recognizing the need for a new, cross-cultural framework, two of this book's authors (Steinfeld and Maisel) developed the eight Goals of Universal Design in 2012. The first four goals – Body Fit, Comfort, Awareness, and Understanding – incorporated research from anthropometry (the study of the size and movements of human bodies), human factors (ergonomics and sensory perception), and the health sciences (e.g., rehabilitation sciences). The fifth goal – Wellness – emerged from growing science on how the materials and forms of products, buildings, and environments affect not only usability but also affect health and well-being. The last three goals – Social Integration, Personalization, and Cultural Appropriateness – leveraged social science research toward the recognition that individuals have diverse needs, preferences, and aspirations, and that norms, taboos, and values differ across geographies and cultures, as do building codes and conventions.

What the current book adds to these outcomes-oriented frameworks is a view of inclusive design *as a process*, rather than as an end product or feature. In other words, architects *practice* inclusive design; they make inclusive designs. The aim of inclusive design, seen through this lens, then, is to identify and refine architectural ways of thinking and working that improve the self-efficacy and self-actualization of all building occupants.

Differences and similarities between inclusive design and two other practices

The development of inclusive design research and practice is contemporaneous with that of sustainability or "green building," and the two share considerable intellectual space. The concept of social sustainability is a sizeable area of overlap. In addition to economic and environmental sustainability, social sustainability provides the third leg or pillar of the current sustainability paradigm. The premise is that a business, institution, or government, or a product, building, or city, cannot be sustained without addressing social equity and justice. Ultimately, social injustices and inequalities will have negative economic and environmental impacts. Another key similarity between inclusive design and green building is the emphasis on design process, including careful thinking about the formation of the design team and its consultants and stakeholders, the sources and research used to guide decisions, and the steps for identifying hidden consequences and improving the likelihood of success. Given their kinship, anecdotal evidence suggests a rising number of clients and architects that are pursuing both inclusive and sustainable design in their projects.

Building codes throughout the developed world, as well as in a growing number of developing countries, include provisions not only for fire safety, structural design, and electrical and plumbing systems, but also for accessibility. Common accessibility codes cover the design of entries, corridors, restrooms, and other spaces particularly for people using wheeled mobility devices, such as wheelchairs. Other codes provide guidance on the design of features for people with visual or hearing impairments. One unintended consequence of accessibility codes, such as Britain's "Part M" or America's "ADAAG," however, was a two-class system of design: one set of solutions for people without disabilities and another for people with disabilities, that is, ceremonial stairs for the former and (non-ceremonial) secondary ramps for the other. Accessibility codes, generally speaking, are a positive result of the Disability Rights movement; access to civic buildings, workplaces, public spaces, housing, and commercial spaces has assuredly improved for people with disabilities living in the United States and Canada, Scandinavia, Korea, Japan, the United Kingdom, and other regions. Mainstreaming disability into design, that is, seeking integrative solutions, is one difference between inclusive design thinking and other methods of meeting accessibility requirements. While their motivations are similar – improving the usability of buildings for diverse users – another subject illustrates a major difference between inclusive design and design for accessibility: aesthetics.

The function and aesthetics of inclusive design

While inclusive design first and foremost needs to be seen as a way of working, it also needs to be viewed from both functional and aesthetic vantage points. Both domains are central to the historic and contemporary practice of architecture. Architecture has often been described as the highest art form, as it is the largest and most spatial art form, involves all sensory domains, and is among the few art forms that involves functionality. Aesthetics is among the largest branches of philosophy but, put simply, is the study of how humans physically and psychologically respond to the artistic, literary, musical, physical, and spatial artifacts and environments they encounter. What we like, what we don't like; what we value, what we devalue; and why and how these conscious and subconscious judgments take place: this is aesthetics.

Aesthetics is often equated to beauty but, particularly for architecture, this definition is too narrow. For architecture, aesthetics encompasses how temperature and humidity, proportion, light and color, acoustics, texture, and a host of other factors make us feel. The judgments we make about buildings also include what we know about the architect or client and how our values align with theirs. How much did the building cost? Who uses it? How well does it function? All these contribute to the cognitive-emotional response we each have to every building we experience. As such, a building that clearly segregates one user group from another communicates a dismissal of the principle of equity and, therefore, may be perceived or experienced negatively not for its material selection, or spatial qualities, or functionality, but for the value system it conveys. Similarly, a building with add-on design elements can be perceived as not well planned, as if each design decision were made in isolation, not part of a cohesive logic. Aesthetics, then, are central, not peripheral, to the inclusive design paradigm.

What are the challenges and rewards of inclusive design?

Over the course of a lifetime, humans' physical, sensory, cognitive abilities, and circumstances dramatically change. This is common and expected, not unusual. The primary challenge for inclusive designers, then, is to build environments that meet people's evolving needs over the course of their entire lives. Given that building practices often meet only the needs of able-bodied adults, the reward for inclusive designers is the expansion of standard practices and the populations they serve.

Human factors

Physical, cognitive, and organizational ergonomics, sometimes called "human factors," addresses the "fit" between users and their environments. Human factors researchers and practitioners consider how context and environment can help or hinder daily work and living. Inclusive design incorporates human factors, seeking to enhance life by reducing health risks and increasing convenience, comfort, safety, and usability. Although the intentions are noble, there are a number of challenges, such as the following:

- Inclusive environments move beyond ergonomic standards. Persuading those who produce and those who use built environments to exceed the standards can be challenging.
- People are not as aware as they could be about how human factors affect quality of life. The public needs more knowledge of human factors principles and the necessity of incorporating them into everyday activities both at work and at home.
- More human factors research is needed to develop a strong evidence base for the design of inclusive environments.

  Despite the challenges, there are many tangible rewards:

- In home design, inclusive approaches make it easier to welcome visitors – parents with babies in strollers, travelers with luggage, those with mobility difficulties, and children who need safe play spaces.
- Inclusive home design facilitates caregiving in the home, which delays the need for institutional living.

- Inclusive workplace design and business practices enable more people to work.
- Workplace design and business practices that follow inclusive principles reduce injuries resulting from repetitive motion, slips/falls, and overexertion.
- Inclusive commercial and retail spaces provide access to a wider range of clients and customers.
- Inclusively designed public spaces allow more people to enjoy public squares, parks, beaches, and other community venues, and encourage a more active lifestyle and social participation.

When designers and manufacturers consider the full range of difficulties that people experience when using products, services, or environments (in other words, they keep accessibility and usability in mind), all people benefit.

Social factors

Social participation, one of the goals of inclusive design, has been linked to improved happiness, health, and well-being. Inclusive designers cannot create participation, but they can create spaces that enable and encourage it. These inclusive environments are especially important for vulnerable and excluded groups who need social involvement to increase their control over decisions that influence health and life quality.[1] Developing social spaces does pose challenges:

- Knowledge gaps still exist regarding an understanding of environmental barriers to socialization and the built features that encourage human bonding. Additional research is needed to determine relationships between design and socialization.
- Establishing safe, inclusive spaces that promote stable social connections is especially challenging in some lower socioeconomic contexts.
- Motivating participation, increasing social trust, and promoting collaboration remains difficult.
- In many situations, social media is replacing physical, space-based socialization and, therefore, reduces physical human contact.
- The increasing reliance on technology for social participation poses risks to people without advanced technologies of being excluded from accessing social opportunities.

Nonetheless, the many existing inclusive solutions that promote socialization promise big rewards, such as the following:

- "Visitability" allows homes to be social spaces rather than places of isolation.
- Workplaces with inclusively designed collaboration spaces promote improved communication between colleagues.
- Public buildings with inclusive components, such as multisensory way-finding cues, intuitive floorplans, and grouped vertical circulation, promote ease of use for all people.
- Inclusively designed public spaces allow people to be more socially connected and civically engaged.
- Technology, which is more embedded into physical environments than ever before, empowers people to become active in communities at all scales.
- Inclusive technologies can be channeled to support community interests such as disaster response, health care, and safety in homes, workplaces, and public spaces.

An inclusive and welcoming atmosphere that fosters social interaction requires designers to be particularly sensitive to the ways and messages that environments communicate. What do various places say about differences of all kinds – cultures, economic statuses, genders, ages, abilities, races, ethnicities, and religions? Are places inviting, or do they set up barriers? Understanding the built environment as part of a social support system can change the ways that designers develop projects. Opportunities to provide spaces for conversation, collaboration, and social change then become a priority.

Economic factors

The financial side of inclusive design can be considered from many scales – building, neighborhood, city, nation, and globe. In addition, financial implications are perceived differently depending on various roles – consumers, builders, developers, manufacturers, urban planners, government officials, and so on. Regardless of scale and role, the business case for inclusive design can present challenges:

- Persuading people about the economic benefits of inclusive design is a difficult proposition because many think that it is more expensive.

Granted, at times, this is the case. However, inclusive design can cost the same as typical projects, and, often, it saves money.

■ Because many of the paybacks of inclusive design are long term, those interested in quick fixes and fast income tend to dismiss its merit.

■ Some builders meet minimum accessibility requirements, but are unwilling to move beyond legal compliance toward inclusive design, even if the cost is the same.

■ Consumer expectations increase with each widely accepted design improvement. While this might be considered a positive, it is also challenging to continually perfect products and built environments without raising costs.

Regardless of the perceived difficulties, the economic rewards of inclusive design are substantial and enduring:

■ If buildings are usable by everyone from the start, then fewer renovations are necessary in the future, thus, saving money for the property owner.

■ Properties that are designed inclusively provide value-added features, which often translate into an increase in resale marketability and return on investment.

■ Given that inclusive design attempts to serve as many people as possible, it follows that it can expand market reach; when products and built environments are made for a wider range of people, the number of potential customers increases.

■ If a product or place is easy to access, easy to use, and simple to understand, educated consumers are more likely to buy it. Inclusive design increases the number of satisfied customers who tell others. Word-of-mouth advertising boosts awareness and potentially creates new clients.

■ Businesses, organizations, and governments that incorporate inclusive design approaches contribute to the betterment of society; as a result, they are establishing reputations as entities that embrace social responsibility.

■ Inclusive design can save money for governments, especially those with federally funded health care. Publicly supported institutionalization fees are greatly reduced if older adults can live in their own inclusively designed homes for longer periods of time. Safer products and environments can reduce injuries and, thus, lower health care bills.

Inclusive design makes good economic sense, especially as populations age. From 2010 to 2050, the world's population is expected to grow by 2 billion people, 1.3 billion being older adults. While some members of this group will have significant buying power, others will rely on public, philanthropic, governmental, and/or familial assistance. Without question, this population growth will have profound economic implications in the coming decades, and inclusive design has the potential to both generate income and save money.[2]

Inclusive design as innovation

Inclusive design ultimately represents an innovative way of thinking about the built environment. Everett Rogers defined an innovation as anything "perceived to be new." Thinking of inclusive design in this way suggests that we can gain insight into the best way to advance its adoption by applying general knowledge about innovation. Based on an exhaustive survey of research on the diffusion of innovations, Rogers proposed that innovation is diffused through a sequence of five activities:

1   Knowledge: exposure to an innovation's existence and some understanding of how it functions;
2   Persuasion: forming "a favorable or unfavorable attitude toward the innovation";
3   Decision: "activities that lead to a choice to adopt or reject the innovation";
4   Implementation: putting "an innovation into use"; and
5   Confirmation: "reinforcement of an innovation-decision already made or reversal of a previous decision to adopt or reject the innovation."[3]

Many experts believe that inclusive design simply means improving regulations. Although necessary, accessible design regulations create the illusion that only people with disabilities need increased usability and safety. This belief has two consequences:

1   Designers perceive that the demand for accessible products and environments is in "niche markets."
2   Providing better access is seen primarily as a regulatory or clinical matter. Thus, designers and producers (manufacturers of products, purveyors

of services, or developers of buildings) believe that it is a problem for a small group of specialists to solve rather than an opportunity for creative design.

Practicing inclusive design, then, requires changing attitudes and perceptions on many levels. Producers need to understand that to be successful in the broader marketplace, products, environments, and services must be easier to use, healthier, and friendlier for people who do not have disabilities, as well as those who do, and they must provide value worth the cost compared with the competition. Products, environments, and services should not only be affordable, but they should also be as attractive, durable, and reliable as their competition.

Knowledge about adoption of innovation, therefore, suggests that two important activities play a major role in adopting inclusive design in practice:

1   Decisions to adopt inclusive design will be heavily influenced by communications (both information in media and face-to-face contact) within and between organizations, industries, professions, and individuals. It is through these communications that awareness is raised and persuasion takes place.
2   Decision-making strategies within an organization and by consumers heavily influence the rate of diffusion. Within organizations, decisions to adopt a new idea are affected by compatibility with company and industry norms; established modes of operation, risks, benefits; and the complexity of implementation. Three factors affect consumer decision making:

    a   The way the innovation is communicated;
    b   Consumer knowledge of product features; and
    c   Consumer assessment of perceived benefits and risks.

Thus, to assess progress in the diffusion of inclusive design as a new idea, these two activities require evaluation. Likewise, inclusive design methods and strategies provide a means for creative problem solving and design innovation.

Notes

1 Abdallah, Saamah, Juliet Michaelson, Sagar Shah, Laura Stoll, and Nic Marks. "The Happy Planet Index: 2012 Report." New Economics Foundation, London, 2012.
2 United Nations, Department of Economic and Social Affairs, Population Division. "World Population Ageing 2015." (ST/ESA/SER.A/390), 2015.
3 Rogers, Everett. *Diffusion of Innovations*. New York, NY: Free Press, p. 169, 1995.

Pre-design

Pre-design, the stage when funding is available and before design begins, is a crucial phase for those in inclusive building practices. While typical pre-design focuses on project vision and goals, programming, site and building analyses, project cost and feasibility, and a review of planning and zoning regulations, inclusive design gives precedence to some of these areas over others. In addition to standard practices, inclusive pre-design involves establishing a diverse project team and making certain that clients and neighborhood communities collaborate with the design team, especially in the planning process. As well, an inclusive designer will spend more time discussing with the client the needs of everyone who will use the space; these include current as well as future needs that engage a wider range of people and circumstances. Furthermore, inclusive designers will devote considerable attention to site and space analysis to ensure ease of site access, seamless circulation, and entry. Focusing on this up front usually results in more integrative solutions that are less expensive. Finally, the environmental, social, political, technological, and economic conditions related to each project require extra planning to guarantee not only inclusive results, but inclusive processes as well. This early investment brings about improved building quality, reduced operational costs, and increased satisfaction among the stakeholders over the life span of the building.

Strategy 1.1   Getting started

At the start of a project, explore and define four elements: (1) the makeup of the project team, (2) the range of potential users and stakeholders and their relationships to one another, (3) the research and site analyses that are most important, and (4) the contextual, yet potentially hidden, factors that might facilitate or impede success.

Who are the stakeholders, what are their roles, and how can they be organized?

Financiers

The financiers of building projects vary depending on the scale and type of development. This group can consist of sponsors; lenders; financial, technical, and legal advisors; equity investors; regulatory agencies; and multilateral agencies. Their primary role is to develop a preliminary assessment of funding options to determine the viability and risks of a project. This assessment most often includes budget, draw-down facilities, approvals and consents, taxes, grants, loan size and term, land value, building costs, end-valuation, stage payments, planning risks, profit on cost, and collateral. Financiers who are backing an inclusively designed project need to clearly understand its vision and goals, how the building will perform differently from conventional buildings, and understand the financial implications of the inclusive design process (i.e., where investments need to be increased, where costs can be saved, and the long-range value of utilizing inclusive design principles).

Building owners and developers

Inclusive design provides building owners and developers with ways to maximize their buildings' responsiveness to an increasingly diverse marketplace. Buildings that are not usable by everyone are becoming more marginalized and, consequently, tend to lose their relative value. Inclusive design has become a cost-effective strategy for maintaining or even enhancing the profitability of building inventories.

Building construction, renovation, and maintenance costs are more readily justified when all people benefit. Consequently, building owners and managers, who embrace the goals of inclusive design, are less likely to see their decision making during construction, renovation, and maintenance projects become the targets of "penny wise and pound foolish" criticisms following their completion.

Architects

Inclusive design is a rapidly expanding area of practice in architecture. The growing need to design buildings that are usable by everyone regardless of their intellectual, functional, or sensory abilities is a demographic fact of life.

Inclusive architects contribute to the socially and ethically responsible design of buildings. They promote replacement of discriminatory exclusive designs with affirming inclusive designs. They understand life cycle requirements and work to enhance the quality of life for every individual through high-performing and aesthetically pleasing spaces that are affordable for all. And, inclusive architects do this without prescriptive standards that might stifle creativity. The benefits of inclusive design are best achieved by reinforcing design innovation rather than design imitation.

General contractors and construction managers

Inclusive design guidelines can help contractors and construction managers develop efficient strategies for responding to both short-term and longer-term conditions encountered during the construction process. More important, the examples and guidelines provide a broad understanding of how application of the principles of inclusive design at a construction site can ensure the realization of a building that is truly usable by everyone – and, typically, at a cost that is competitive with conventional design and construction methods. Contractors and construction managers require specialized knowledge of inclusive construction practices such as how to install French drains at no-step entrances and dropped shower floor pans in roll-in showers. They are responsible for ensuring that the infrastructure for future inclusive features (e.g., blocking for grab bars and stacked closets with reinforced walls for eventual elevators) is included as part of standard building construction.

Facility managers

A well-functioning built environment requires integration of people, places, processes, and technology. Inclusive integration of these elements necessitates a deeper understanding of the potential ways that marginalized groups interact with the environment. While all facility managers organize and oversee buildings and their premises, inclusive practitioners place special focus on human factors; multisensory communication; emergency preparedness for all occupants, especially those with disabilities; accessible space planning; environmental health and safety; and administering essential inclusive services (reception, security, maintenance, cleaning, recycling, etc.). Their management at both the strategic planning and day-to-day operation levels requires specific goals developed in concert with building occupants followed by regular evaluation of progress.

Above all, inclusive facility managers need to consider lasting solutions to complex problems even though they might take longer to develop. Anticipating the unintended consequences of building operations requires input from all people who use the building; that way, causes of problems are favored over treating mere symptoms.

Building servicers

Most building servicers are responsible for the installation, management, and monitoring of the systems required for the safe, comfortable, and sustainable operation of buildings. Inclusive servicers differ in that they seek regular feedback from building superintendents and occupants to ensure that the integrated systems are working smoothly at all times. In addition, they use inclusive design principles and goals both to determine the best systems and recurrently evaluate them once installed. Comfortable spaces and temperature, clean air, ample lighting, efficient communication and power capabilities, high-quality sanitation, accessible pathways and vertical circulation, and protection of life and property are the primary foci of inclusive servicers.

Clients

Regardless of whether clients are purchasing office buildings or a single-family home, they want to customize spaces to meet current and future needs. The spatial configurations, features, materials, and products they choose can further this goal. Understanding the principles and goals of inclusive design can help clients make thoughtful decisions that accommodate occupants' changing requirements. Educated clients purchase inclusively designed elements that are integrated and virtually invisible. An essential part of their charge involves in-depth planning that considers all potential users and uses for the space. This calls for more work up front, but raises the quality of choices and, thus, the performance and efficiency of the built environment.

End users

Inclusive living is the responsibility of all who are part of a building's life cycle. End users play a critical role in ensuring the best possible environment. However, to actively participate, most need education in inclusive design practices. Occupants require accurate, up-to-date information on the benefits of inclusive living, including aspects for which they have direct control such as placement of freestanding furniture, task lighting, and handheld objects;

elimination of toxic chemicals and allergens; and setup of multisensory functions on communication devices. Empowering end users by making them aware of specific actions they can take to improve the functions of the building provides consistent, on-site attention. As part of the team who reports building-related inclusive design inefficiencies to building management, occupants assume stewardship of their environment.

How does research in preparation for an inclusive project differ from traditional research processes?

Research is an integral part of any design process. Evidence-based design is a growing field in planning, the design professions, and construction, where credible research is used to influence design decisions. Designers, builders, and developers use available information from a variety of resources, including precedent studies, user input, project evaluations, and targeted research studies to improve efficacy and performance outcomes such as safety, usability, and cost. Evidence-based design has become commonplace for health care facilities and other projects that tend to be high in cost, that require specialized knowledge and consultants, and where design oversights possess catastrophic consequences. When preparing for any project, at minimum, research needs to incorporate findings from similar projects and include data on the specific users of the building. For an inclusive project, research must also include data from diverse stakeholder groups; a successful inclusive project gathers information on a wide spectrum of users, including those individuals at the extremes of the "bell curve."

Anthropometric dimensions taken from a large enough population will distribute themselves in a normal distribution or bell curve (see Figure 1.1). Most people will fall in the middle part of the curve (within two standard deviations from the mean), with very few at either of the extremes. The rationale for not accommodating everyone's needs in a design project is usually that it is not cost effective to do so because most people will fall in the middle part of the curve; clearly, this general rule does not address the Goals of Universal Design. The first objective of any design project should be to try and accommodate everyone. When design for the extremes is not feasible, a more realistic target is addressing the needs of the 5th–95th percentiles.

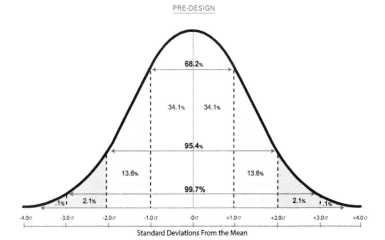

1.1 Normal distribution bell curve

When it is apparent that some people will have to be excluded, the 5th–95th rule can be applied to the *population group that is most likely to be excluded by a design*. For example, enough space can be allocated to accommodate the 95th percentile of maneuvering abilities for *wheeled mobility device users*. If their needs are met, it is likely that all ambulatory individuals will have enough space as well.[1]

    Rarely does an individual fit within the same range for every characteristic or ability. A person with a long trunk may have short arms, or a person with short stature may have large hands. Since two different dimensions taken from the same person may represent different percentile values within the population, there is no such thing as a person who can serve as a model user for the 5th or 95th percentile. Each design has to be addressed separately using research data on the related anthropometric parameter from a representative sample of the end user population, if that information is available.

Precedent studies
When embarking on a new project, designers, builders, and other stakeholders may benefit from researching and referencing precedents. Precedent studies are earlier occurrences of similar projects that can serve as examples for guiding design decisions. For example, they can help identify both successful and unsuccessful strategies that can be applied or avoided in a new

project. Using precedent studies lends authority to a specific design and offers an opportunity to communicate potential designs to key stakeholders. The ability to demonstrate the construction practices, materials, or style from an existing project allows stakeholders such as investors, clients, and end users the ability to more accurately understand a project. When selecting an appropriate precedent study, it is important to understand the current design problem and select a suitable model that addresses a similar problem. Wherever possible, it is also important to utilize precedents that successfully incorporate the needs and wants of diverse groups and support desirable performance outcomes. *UDNY, UDNY2, The Universal Design Handbook, Universal Design: Creating Inclusive Environments, The Inclusive City*, and so forth are just a few of the resources that provide precedents for housing, commercial building, transportation, and product-related projects that incorporate the needs of a variety of end users. Despite the benefits of referencing precedents, it remains important to acknowledge that sometimes breaking with precedents leads to innovative solutions that may benefit everyone.

In contrast to precedent studies, case studies offer in-depth investigations of a specific topic that describes and/or evaluates a real-life project or process. Case studies typically bring to light exemplary projects and concepts worthy of replication or broader dissemination. They often serve to formalize what are typically generalizations or anecdotal information about projects and processes.

User input: survey, focus groups, etc.

A critical aspect of research in pre-design is to learn from the people who will use, visit, and manage the building/site. The aim is to support and enhance their independence, productivity, and satisfaction. Gathering user input can occur using a variety of research methods, such as observations, focus groups, surveys, and interviews. Each method offers advantages and disadvantages in gaining information and perspectives.

Strategy 1.2   Gathering useful information

Utilize multiple sources of information and leverage an array of methods for gathering it, including observation, focus groups, surveys, and interviews of clients, occupants, and other stakeholders.

Observations are a helpful first step in data gathering because they provide useful information on how occupants interact with one another and the built environment in their existing setting. More specifically, direct observations enable the designer to understand both who is using the space and how they are using it, including patterns and anomalies of activity, individual preferences and needs, and high- and low-functioning spaces and features. Oftentimes, users are unable to describe their needs and/or requirements when they are asked. Observations allow designers to gather more information than they might otherwise have if they simply just interviewed users. Whereas users may be non-forthcoming in interviews or focus groups, observations allow designers to see users perform activities in a natural setting. Thus, designers are able to see how things are really done. Observations, however, can be time consuming. Also, they may not reveal important information if specific activities did not occur during the designated observation times or if the act of observing disrupts normal routines.

Focus groups are useful when it is unclear what the primary issues are, when a variety of opinions are needed, and/or when detailed information on a specific issue is desired. A focus group facilitator can guide the conversation and probe for more details and/or more useful information. Including focus groups helps the design team gather more specific information from different user groups. Having a group of people in the same room often leads to opinions and ideas that arise more easily than in individual interviews. Often confused, a focus group is not simply a more efficient method of interviewing and gathering the input of many people in a short time. The reason for a focus group, rather than one-on-one interviewing, is to gain knowledge not only about the *topic* of the conversation, but also about the *dynamics* of the conversation – the exchange, debate, and evolution of ideas. Successful focus groups often have at least two facilitators: one person who focuses on guiding the discussion and encouraging discussion among all participants and the other person to focus on recording information. Since there are often multiple people with rich discussions taking place, recording a focus group is a good practice. Facilitators need a plan for the topics to be discussed, but also must provide flexibility to accommodate both a natural flow in the conversation and emergent, unanticipated discussion topics.

Surveys are most effective when a little information about many topics is needed and when the people responding are likely interested enough to take the time to complete the survey. They are also a useful tool when people might find it uncomfortable to respond to a specific question in front of others. Surveys often occur with a larger sample and when the goal is to gather a lot of information quickly. Therefore, calculating the frequency of specific answers provides a sense of the strength of agreement among respondents. Surveys should not be used to acquire tremendous details. Modern technology has made this type of communication much easier and more direct. Through the use of an online survey, a large sample may be selected and questioned easily compared with other methods, and usually with minimal impact on that selected sample. To employ a proper online survey, an appropriate and reliable survey generator must first be selected. Examples of such software include SurveyMonkey and Google Docs. Carefully select the questions to include in any survey. Things to consider include question content, response formats (e.g., multiple choice, rating scale), and how to appropriately word the question so it is both clear and unbiased.

Face-to-face, structured, or semi-structured interviews are another suitable data gathering method for obtaining opinions and needs from specific stakeholders. It allows the interviewer to have a purposeful conversation with the user. A semi-structured interview format, with open- and closed-ended questions, as well as allowances to enter parallel topics of discussion or to probe more deeply via follow-up questions, provides both structure and flexibility. While the interviewer often starts with a skeletal script and a set of general topics to cover during the interview session, which then can be used in other interviews for consistency, he or she seeks clarification or elaboration on information that is either intriguingly new or critical to the project. Semi-structured interviews yield rich, detailed information; however, the information obtained may not be representative of all user groups and, therefore, may not be generalizable beyond that one interviewee. As such, interviewers utilize techniques that cross compare the information collected from various interviewees. Analyzing the notes or transcripts from all interviewees and developing cross-cutting "themes" or "stories" is common practice. These themes, as well as quotes or excerpts, can also be shared back with all interviewees to gauge accuracy and identify the degree of consensus. (Note: consensus building is not the aim; divergent opinions are common and do not need to be cast aside.)

It is also possible, often recommended, to use multiple methods of collecting information. Using surveys, interviews, and focus groups in concert can help the architectural team discern which themes or priorities carry the most weight and which are of secondary or tertiary importance. For example, focus groups can uncover some key issues, which can then be applied to create a more targeted and meaningful survey. Likewise, if survey results are confusing, and/or inconsistent, focus groups can then clarify some of the irregularities and provide more details.

Several additional concepts from qualitative research are worth noting. *Reflexivity* is the conscientious awareness of the effects of the interviewer – that the interviewer, by her or his demeanor, mannerisms, word choices, and responses, can influence the responses of the interviewee. While an architect-client interview is a two-way conversation and reciprocal exchange of information, architects need to be mindful of their own affectations. Architects might also look to the techniques used in other disciplines. *Motivational interviewing*, for example, is commonly used in clinical health care settings, where the physician or therapist is assisting the client to improve physical or mental health through behavior or lifestyle changes. The specific tactics of motivational interviewing, on which a great deal has been written, can be applied to an architectural practice setting; particularly for projects seeking to fulfill inclusive design goals, the larger tenets of motivational interviewing – collaboration, empowerment, and transformation – may be most useful. The architect, client, and end users compose a collaborative team; the role of the architect is to empower the client and end users; and this process transforms the thinking of all three collaborators.

In effect, as the design team gathers information from multiple sources through multiple methods, they are deploying three complementary concepts of qualitative research. The first, *triangulation*, is a process of seeking multiple points of information in order to substantiate or refine themes as they emerge. The second, *validation*, seeks to affirm and deepen the accuracy and broad applicability of information. With clients, this can come in the form of follow-up interviews, where clients are presented summaries of previous conversations. The third, *saturation*, is the point at which no new information will be gleaned from conducting further interviews, surveys, focus groups, or precedent studies. It signals to the design team that it is time to move on in the pre-design process.

Using foundational and targeted research

Foundational and targeted research provide additional opportunities to learn about a building's intended users. Foundational research strives to uncover more information about the users, including their mental models (i.e., how they view things working), motivations, and goals. Targeted research focuses on specific issues that have emerged from broader research. It addresses knowledge gaps and seeks to answer more focused questions. Examples of targeted research may include specific anthropometric studies related to a building's use and its users. In building design, anthropometry is critical for ensuring user safety and convenience. For instance, building regulations specify the minimum widths of emergency egress routes, including hallways and doors. These regulations are based on body size, including adjustments for the way people move in groups, with implications such as the width of exit openings needed to ensure a fast flow of people in an emergency. Other applications of functional anthropometry include identifying the size of a railing that can be grasped quickly when needed, planning the amount of space needed for seating circulation and serving in a dining area of a restaurant, determining where a switch or outlet should be placed to be within convenient reach, and identifying how much clear space is needed in a doorway to accommodate wheelchair users. Designers can benefit from knowledge of functional anthropometry for programming, planning furniture arrangements, and locating signs in their facilities. Targeted research may also include studies that examine user preferences.

Ultimately, gaining a full picture of a design problem requires both research and design thinking. Research needs to include the following:

■ Collecting demographic and statistical trends on the community or region within which the building resides;

■ Reviewing municipal, state, and national codes and laws that empower or protect various demographic groups, and the implications of these policies for design; and

■ Reviewing usability studies of recently built and historic buildings in the area.

Creative approaches might include the following:

■ Meeting with community leaders and community-based organizations, particularly human-rights groups;

■ Meeting with academics doing civic outreach projects in the region;

■ Design team ideation, that is, group brainstorming on the widest range of possible users;

■ Questioning the conventions of design from foundational human fac-tors standpoints, such as anthropometry, sensory perception, and human cognition;

■ An ongoing quest for empowering otherwise marginalized groups, con-tinually asking, Who are we not thinking about?; and

■ Analogical reasoning, which uses knowledge from an unrelated field, such as biology or geology, and applies it to a design context.

While this is by no means an exhaustive list of creative approaches to research, all these examples seek to uncover hidden needs and aspirations among diverse, prospective user groups.

What are the primary issues in site selection and analysis for an inclusive design project?

Zoning

Local zoning codes must be considered and understood when selecting a proj-ect site. Zoning is an element of land use planning that local governments employ to control how pieces of land are used and what building types are constructed on the land. In some instances, zoning encourages targeted devel-opment, whereas in other instances, zoning is used to prevent specific types of development. Zoning practices continue to evolve as legal restrictions, political priorities, and planning theory all change. The various approaches to zoning can be divided into four broad categories: Euclidean, performance-based, incentive-based, and form-based.

1   Euclidean zoning segregates land uses into specified geographic districts and outlines prescriptive requirements that specify development activity within a district type. Advantages include ease of implementation and familiarity. However, Euclidean zoning has received criticism for its lack of flexibility and reliance on outdated planning practices.

2   Performance-based zoning uses goal-oriented criteria to establish param-eters for proposed development projects. Although not widely used in the United States, performance zoning is intended to provide flexibility, transparency, and accountability.

3   Incentive-based zoning provides a reward-based system to encourage development that meets established urban development goals. This zoning method seeks to entice developers to incorporate the desired development criteria. Incentive zoning allows for a high degree of flexibility, but can be complex to administer.

4   Form-based zoning regulates not the type of land use, but the form that land use may take. For instance, form-based zoning in a dense area may insist on short setbacks, high density, and pedestrian accessibility. Form-based codes are context sensitive and directly respond to the physical structure of a community.[2]

Case study 1.1 – The SmartCode

The SmartCode is an example of a form-based code that incorporates Smart Growth and New Urbanist principles. The SmartCode uses transects – cross-section diagrams through critical functions, spaces, and ecologies – to illustrate six categories, or prototypical zones, of land use based on density, ranging from natural environments to urban cores. The six transect zones (T-zones) provide the basis for neighborhood design, including walkable streets, mixed-use, transportation systems, and housing diversity (see Figure 1.2). The T-zones vary by the ratio and level of intensity of their natural, built, and social components. The six T-zones can be described as follows:

1   *T1 Natural* includes parklands, wilderness areas, and wetlands that are permanently protected from development.

2   *T2 Rural* is the countryside – where development may occur but where it may not be encouraged. Public infrastructure is sparse or nonexistent in the rural zone. The rural zone can be protected from development through mechanisms such as transfer of development rights, land banks, and agricultural zoning.

3   *T3 Suburban* represents the context of a first ring suburb, but it is also characteristic of single-family neighborhoods within

city limits. Detached houses on streets designed to balance convenient use of vehicles with pedestrian needs are typical in this zone. Vehicular access to lots could occur from the street or alleys. Off-street parking is provided on each lot for more than one car. Services, access to public transportation, and recreation facilities would be located within walking distance. Apartments in this zone are accessory units such as carriage houses or are located in small buildings that look similar to large houses. Lot sizes are relatively large with ample setbacks, and most lots have driveways. There are sidewalks at the sides of all streets. Some streets may be cul-de-sacs off feeder streets.

4   *T4 General Urban* represents residential neighborhoods with a higher density. Here, a mixture of housing types is found. Streets accommodate vehicles but they are designed to favor pedestrians. Vehicle access to individual lots is usually limited to curbside or to the rear of the lots. More commercial and civic facilities are available in this zone than in the T3 zone. The houses include a range from large, single-family, detached types on larger lots to higher density, single-family buildings like attached houses or townhouses and small apartment buildings. Setbacks are minimal. Civic and commercial land uses are provided on major streets. There may be some mixed-use buildings like live-work units. Parkways or boulevards integrate recreational spaces with streetscapes. There may be squares and mews interspersed in the urban fabric.

5   *T5 Urban Center* features mixed-use buildings on pedestrian-friendly commercial streets. Parking is provided on the street or on the site in lots or in garages. There may be neighborhood garages that serve houses within walking distance. Density is higher than in the T4 zone and there are more commercial and civic land uses. There are no single-family detached dwellings or small apartment buildings. High-density low-rise buildings are the most common building form. Setbacks are minimal or nonexistent. Commercial land uses are more extensive, and

mixed-use buildings are common in commercial areas. All streets have sidewalks, but park strips and boulevards are less common. Urban squares and piazzas may be provided.

6   *T6 Urban Core* is the densest and most urban part of the human environment. Many cities have only one core, often known as the downtown. The core is a focal point of activity and energy, benefiting from substantial traffic – both pedestrian and automotive. Buildings in the core are highly flexible in their uses – commonly mixing uses with shops and businesses on the first floor, and offices or residential units above.[3]

NATURAL | RURAL | SUBURBAN | GENERAL URBAN | URBAN CENTER | URBAN CORE

1.2 Urban transect

Transportation systems and connectivity

Transportation plays an essential role in creating an inclusive society. In mobile, global cultures, full social participation hinges on accessibility of transportation systems, at both community and intercity scales. Transportation systems provide access to many opportunities, especially employment. One of the main barriers to employment, education, and social participation is simply access to services. This takes three forms: lack of any public transportation in one's neighborhood, lack of the ability to pay for service, and the presence of design barriers. In highly developed countries, one of the most underserved groups in transportation is people with disabilities.

A convenient, easy-to-use, safe, and effective public transportation system contributes substantially to the long-term health of a city – by supporting environmental, economic, and social sustainability. The inclusive design of transportation benefits not only citizens of the community but also visitors. From an economic perspective, it encourages trade and tourism and can play an important role in business location decisions. All passengers in a transportation system stand to benefit from inclusive design by improving resources used to plan trips, providing access to the system, and reducing barriers and stress during trips. In fact, inclusive design also benefits transportation providers by reducing workload, increasing rider self-sufficiency, reducing operating and maintenance costs, and increasing ridership. Thus, everyone shares in the investment.

Connectivity for everyone to everywhere is the test for effective planning and design. Strategies that encourage connectivity include the following:

- Reducing distances to neighborhood resources via pedestrian paths, for example, paths that cut across blocks;
- Facilitating access to street crossings and public transportation stops for people with a wide range of functional limitations; and
- Installing site furniture, such as benches, seating walls, bus shelters, and lighting that support a wide range of needs and are located to support social interaction.

Land use planning is critical for establishing connectivity and developing inclusive communities. Since World War II, land use practices, particularly in the United States and some European countries, have focused on the segregation of functions and uses, for example, separating commercial and residential areas. These practices have been used extensively in suburban development, as well as in the redevelopment of older cities. The practice has now extended to some rapidly developing south Asian and sub-Saharan African cities. This has created barriers to accessibility for all citizens. Combined with huge subsidies for road construction and free parking, this has led to great dependence on automobile transportation for daily mobility except in some inner-city urban areas like New York City and San Francisco.

Segregation of housing types based on lot size restrictions and exclusive zoning for single- and multifamily development has resulted in segregation of social groups based on income and ability to obtain financing for home ownership. In suburban development, apartments are usually walk-up garden apartments. In the United States, nearly all of these apartments had stairs leading to them, even the first-floor units, until the Fair Housing Amendments Act went into effect in 1991. Concerns about housing inaccessibility in the United Kingdom led to the concept of Lifetime Homes. Developed in the early 1990s by housing experts, including Habinteg Housing Association and the Joseph Rowntree Foundation, Lifetime Homes incorporates sixteen Design Criteria that can be applied to new homes at minimal cost to increase their accessibility.[4]

Street patterns also play an important role in inclusive design. The proliferation of major arterials with four to six lanes of traffic creates barriers to street crossing and makes pedestrian activity dangerous and unhealthy. Even in local neighborhoods, design features like large radius curbs, gated communities with single entries, feeder and collector streets, extensive use of cul-de-sacs, and lack of sidewalks facilitate high-speed automobile travel, increased walking distances, and create hazardous conditions for people who do not drive, including children, wheeled mobility device users, and cyclists (see Figure 1.3).

Complete streets

The complete streets (CS) approach to right-of-way (ROW) design emerged due to a shift in transportation planning, which started to encourage a

1.3 Non-pedestrian friendly street design

prioritization of non-automotive travel modes and the needs of diverse user groups when planning, building, operating, and maintaining community transportation systems. The CS approach encourages changes to planning efforts that balance the needs of pedestrians, bicyclists, public transportation users, and motorists, regardless of age, ability, income, ethnicity, or mode of travel. The community benefits of the CS approach include urban revitalization, traffic calming, improved pedestrian safety, reduced vehicle usage and the concomitant fuel consumption and greenhouse gas emissions, improved population health due to increases in walking and bicycling, and improved access to daily services for older adults and people with disabilities.[5]

CS policies have been adopted by state governments and agencies, regional organizations, and individual municipalities, and often incorporate different criteria to guide planning, decision making, and funding allocation; project implementation; and evaluation. While CS initiatives may result in ROW designs that include curb cuts, crosswalks with pedestrian refuge

1.4 McDonald's with turquoise arches in Sedona, Arizona
Photo by Doug Kerr

islands, bike lanes, and landscaping that enhances the pedestrian experience, CS projects are likely to look very different from city to city since CS policies often do not mandate specific prescriptive design solutions.

Neighborhood context

Regardless of the policies in place, establishing and preserving neighborhood character are important goals of urban design, as well as inclusive urban design. The form of natural features, land uses, streets, blocks, lots, and buildings determines the overall character of a neighborhood and need to be preserved and respected during design and construction. For example, due to differences in climate, topography, history, and culture, appropriate designs for the southwest region of the United States will and should look very different to designs found in the northeast (see Figure 1.4).

What is inclusive programming, and how does it differ from typical programming?

A building "program" is often equated, though rather loosely, to the set of functions, uses, or activities of a building. More holistically, programming is the act of interpreting the client's goals and preferences, identifying the end user's needs and expectations, and hearing the aspirations and concerns of other stakeholders, all of which is used to define priorities for the project, the hierarchy of decisions and decision makers, and the overarching design process. For many architectural projects, particularly smaller commercial or residential buildings, programming emphasizes the client or patron's point of view. For larger mixed-use, civic, or institutional projects, other constituencies are commonly included. In both cases, from a standpoint of inclusion, a "polyvocal" (multiple voices) approach is important.

Project goals, scope, and feasibility

Prior to programming, the first steps in any project involve defining the project goals, outlining the project scope, and identifying any feasibility challenges. What is the purpose of the project? What do the developers and building owners hope to achieve through the project? Who is the target population? A clear set of goals will help with decision making throughout the design and construction process. Once the design team and building owner establish the project's overarching goals, they must define the project scope. The project scope extends beyond the physical footprint of the proposed building. It refers to (1) the entire physical area that the project will impact, and (2) the various phases of design and construction that the project addresses. Consequently, designers need to think in a more thoughtful way about the relationship of a specific project/building to the surrounding area. A beautiful, inclusively designed building means nothing if access to amenities, transportation, and so forth are not considered. The project scope also addresses more than just the physical footprint and construction process. A successful project utilizes a life cycle perspective with a project scope that includes pre-design, design, construction, and post-occupancy phases.

Even with clear project goals and a defined scope, executing a project may not always be feasible. Feasibility refers to the potential project limitations. What are the building codes and policies in place that promote or set up barriers to achieving inclusive design? What financial limitations exist that might influence decision making? A successful project examines not only the short-term financial feasibility, but also long-term feasibility. Considering initial costs alone is not sufficient. To convince buyers that an additional investment in innovative practices (e.g., sustainability, inclusive design) is worthwhile and advantageous in the long run, stakeholders should instead consider the life cycle costs of a building. This includes the initial costs along with maintenance costs, upgrading costs, and so forth. Factoring that into an inclusive design differentiates it from traditional design practices.

Client goals and preferences

Each client, or patron, comes to a project with a set of goals for the project. The client might be experienced in leading design or development projects, or it might be the first project of the client. In either case, the goals may be well articulated or rather vague. Architects and their teams, therefore, need to possess not only structural, spatial, material, and construction knowledge, but also strong interviewing skills. While client interviews (and/or surveys) are common practice, and often kick off a project, beginning with informal conversations and culminating in a contract, many architects are not taught or aware of the variety of tested interviewing techniques or the implications of various techniques. The personalities, emotional states, biases, and attributes (e.g., gender, age, life experiences) of both the interviewer (architect) and interviewee (client) shape the conversation and can, therefore, shape the building. In a project or team utilizing an inclusive design approach, gathering information from clients and stakeholders is essential. Interviews and other methods need to uncover not only the explicit and tacit goals of the interviewees, but also how secondary influences such as education, culture, or personal beliefs affect building design, embracing the value that they bring, or anticipating and countering possible negative consequences.

Diverse users, diverse needs

While sustainability in architecture is often discussed along the lines of environmental impacts, the sustainability – longevity – of a building is highly determined by its flexibility in accommodating multiple functions and occupants over time. An architect, therefore, needs to not only design for the immediate future, the inaugural tenants of a building, but also anticipate future scenarios. Central to scenario building during the programming phase is to think broadly and creatively about all the different people who might use a building – people with visual or hearing impairments, children and their grandparents, native-language speakers and their non-fluent counterparts, and so forth. The aspiration is for the architecture to reflect and accommodate the diversity of society now and in the future. A classic case where building design misrepresents society is the design of restroom facilities based on binary (male vs. female) thinking. This has proven problematic not only for people whose gender identity resides outside this binary, but also for parents assisting children of the opposite sex and caregivers providing assistance to older adults or people with disabilities of the opposite sex. Thinking creatively about the unique circumstances of various users allows the architect to design for the needs of nursing mothers as well as people using mobility aids, victims of abuse as well as people with service animals, people with learning disabilities, as well as individuals from diverse religious or ethnic backgrounds.

From purpose to use to empowerment

Programming entails multiple phases and incorporates several scales of thinking. At the highest level, according to architectural theorist Richard Hill, are the "purpose" and "function" of a building, while "uses" and "activities" are part of the finer-grained aspects of programming. Using Hill's example, the *purpose* of a school is to facilitate the education of children; the *function* is to provide shelter, safety, and space for learning; and *uses* and *activities* include reading, writing, group discussion, physical education, and music and art education, to name a few, along with supporting activities such as eating and play. Architects, clients, and stakeholders work together to define the purpose and function of a building, and then articulate the uses and activities that facilitate achieving those aims.

For projects that seek greater user satisfaction and social inclusion, an additional framework is needed to complement these phases of programming. How can the building not only support the functions and activities that occur inside and outside it, but also how can the building empower a higher level of human performance, satisfaction, and attainment? In the case of a school, how can spatial organization, proportions, materials, lighting, and acoustics foster learning, particularly for students with the greatest educational challenges? Urban schools in the United States, for example, often serve economically and ethnically diverse populations – students who speak a variety of languages, who come from varied family structures and income levels, and who practice an array of religious customs or cultural traditions. These schools also host students on the autism spectrum, students with hearing impairments, students with cerebral palsy, students with allergies, students who are color blind, and students with attention deficit disorder – a nearly innumerable expanse of human diversity – while also serving as community centers, temporary shelters, and a host of secondary functions. Schools in cities across the United States and abroad, therefore, serve as essential pieces of neighborhood infrastructure, empowering their students and community members to achieve their greatest potential. Without it, individual, household, neighborhood, and citywide success would be diminished. Schools, hospitals, and civic buildings may be the clearest examples, but designing apartment buildings, offices, and commercial spaces also benefit by keeping in mind the vast array of user groups that might occupy an architectural work. The market base of the apartment building widens; the employee prospect pool expands, just as employee productivity is enhanced for the office building; and, for the commercial building, the number of potential tenants and consumers increases. In all cases, designing from the standpoint of both functionality and empowerment improves marketability and long-term sustainability.

Occupancy demands

Designing for social diversity and individual empowerment is the founding premise of inclusive programming. This broad mission, however, also needs to be complemented with the specific programming considerations of each project that is commonplace to this phase of architectural design. Occupancy type is the leading consideration, as it has fire code and other implications. Each occupancy classification – for example, residential, industrial, educational – comes with a set of explicit or implied uses and activities. In addition to meeting the code requirements for these activities, designing from the standpoint of inclusion necessitates a deeper investigation into the range of user groups, the diversity within each user group, the various activities that occur, and the range of ways that users carry out those activities.

In a concert hall, for example, the audience is the primary user group, but the architect must also design from the standpoint of performers, administrative staff, and technical and customer service staff. Across these groups, one can expect a range of ages, physical and sensory abilities, and needs. Therefore, the design team must consider the variety of ways that the audience, performers, and staff move, see, listen, and interact. How can the concert hall accommodate both hearing and non-hearing audiences? How can it meet the needs of both ambulatory and non-ambulatory musicians? How can the design of wayfinding systems complement the work of customer service staff in assisting people with and without cognitive or visual impairments? And how can less obvious design elements, such as ventilation and thermal comfort systems, accommodate the needs of older adults and people with health conditions that affect the regulation of body temperature? Many questions are covered by occupancy codes, while others are not as explicit. Inclusive design seeks to unearth those design factors that are less commonly articulated in building codes, but that have significant impacts on occupants' experiences and satisfaction.

Spatial hierarchy

As questions like those previously mentioned are answered, the pre-design phase arrives at a critical threshold, where the aspirations of the work, that is, meeting client goals and occupancy demands, are made architectural. This is a translational moment, when verbal concepts and values are transformed into a structural, spatial, and material language. At this juncture, the risk is that the research into best practices, the stakeholder interviews, the brainstorming, and lessons learned get lost in the translational process. The design team needs to compare what is emerging in sketch form with what was articulated throughout the programming process, asking, Is the emerging design a direct outgrowth of the inclusive programming process? In what ways do the lessons learned and the emergent schemes mirror one another (or not)?

Spatial hierarchy is a top priority at this point, as it, of course, affects structural and other decisions, many of which have budgetary implications. In addition, as seen from an inclusive design standpoint, spatial organization – including the size, proportion, and proximity of spaces, as well as circulation patterns and thresholds – imparts the foundation for mobility, accessibility, wayfinding, thermal comfort, acoustics, and other experiential factors. Nevertheless, in design, choices need to be made. Not all client goals, user needs, or design elements will achieve the same importance or quality. Aligning the budget, therefore, with the emergent design of the project is a key consideration.

What budget factors are important for an inclusive design project?

The first question that someone unfamiliar with inclusive design will ask when they hear about it is, "What will it cost?" But, although cost is important, this is the wrong question to ask. There is the old adage, "You get what you pay for." In all economic transactions, the most important issue is value. A person should be asking, "What is the economic benefit of adopting inclusive design?" Of course, cost always is important because most projects have a finite budget. But there are priorities in every project as well. Value orientations are embedded in the fabric of the environment. The most obvious examples are religious buildings like the Gothic cathedrals and their modern-day equivalents, sporting palaces, and landmark arts venues. In all these cases, vast sums of public money were invested with dubious economic returns. Research and experience show that accessibility features cost less than 1% of new construction costs. Inclusive design features may cost more but, unless they are mandated by law, they can be selected strategically to address important project priorities that have high value to the owner, inhabitants, and visitors.[6]

In some cases, the value of inclusive design features is obvious. In a supermarket, for example, no one questions the installation of expensive automated doors because they obviously benefit everyone, including employees, and they have direct economic benefits because they reduce congestion at entries, accidents, and the need for staff to help customers. All these impacts can be quantified. In other cases, value is not so easy to quantify in the design phase. Hard decisions often have to be made without good information. The "social capital" invested in a project is often overlooked in making decisions about priorities. For example, in a small project like a bus shelter, the design team must make decisions about the resources. What will be the best investment for the project, increased levels of comfort and security or a more iconic form? Although both are difficult to quantify, the former produces more social capital because it can lead to increased ridership and revenue, as well as greater support for future investments in public transportation by demonstrating that an agency cares about the user's experience.

False choices are often presented as arguments against the adoption of inclusive design. In the previous bus shelter example, the choice to spend money on comfort and security versus iconic form is actually a false one, since iconic form does not necessarily increase costs. A creative design team can find a way to produce iconic form for very little cost, if any. Another type of false choice hinges on a bureaucratic argument. For example, "Including companion restrooms will increase costs because we will be adding plumbing fixtures to the project." This argument arises from the fact that some codes still require a minimum number of fixtures in men's and women's bathrooms based on overall building size and uses, without making allowances for companion restrooms. But reasonable code officials understand that the fixtures in companion restrooms actually are more efficient than in the gender-segregated bathrooms and will readily provide waivers from the obsolete requirements.

Thus, when introducing inclusive design to someone unfamiliar with its practice, it is best to talk about *value proposition* rather than cost. The value of inclusive design should be brought up even before the inevitable question about cost is raised. Make it clear that inclusive design is not about add-on features that cost more but, instead, about finding a better balance in priorities, increasing value over the long term, and increasing investment in social capital. It is also important to emphasize that there is no law that mandates inclusive design like there is for accessible design, so there is a choice of which features to include. Finally, it is important not to confuse the cost of mandated accessibility features with inclusive design features. The former must be provided anyway, therefore they are not part of the cost of inclusive design. For example, larger clearances for wheelchair access should be provided in inclusive design practice, but the real cost is not the entire clearance, just the marginally increased clearance. Accessibility codes may require a 60 in (1525 mm) turning radius, but for inclusive design, 68 in (1730 mm) is desirable. The marginal cost for the additional 8 in (205 mm) is the cost of inclusive design in this case, and it is likely to be insignificant.

Feasibility study

The adoption of inclusive design begins with a project feasibility study. Even at this early stage of a project, it is possible to identify the key inclusive design features desired so they can be made a priority in the initial design development. For example, Congregation Beit Simchat Torah, a synagogue in New York City serving the lesbian, gay, bisexual, and transgender community, was concerned about both hate crimes and terrorism. They did not want to make their new facility a fortress that would discourage participation and stigmatize the building. They also lost a large percentage of their membership to the AIDS epidemic in the 1980s and 1990s. They included blast proof glass exterior walls to protect the inhabitants from explosive devices and a special commemorative wall to remember members who passed away. Although expensive, these features were an integral part of the project. They demonstrate a priority put on investments of social capital rather than on investments made on a purely monetary basis.

Case study 1.2 – Access Living Chicago

Inclusive design features are often useful in helping to raise money, obtain other contributions, and get buy-in from key decision makers. Access Living Chicago, an independent living center and advocacy organization serving the Chicago region, built a new headquarters in Chicago, Illinois. They have a very high proportion of people with disabilities as employees, and they serve a clientele with widely diverse needs. The design team identified many high-cost items that were desirable to include in the building. An air purification system could provide very good indoor air quality for employees and visitors who had chemical sensitivities. Since they have many wheelchair users on staff and the building site demanded a multistory building, more elevators than typically required for a building of that size would be appropriate, along with special provisions for emergency egress. Finally, the site had limited parking, so a garage would be desirable to provide some minimum accessible parking and a weather-protected loading area. These and other features meant that the target cost of the building would be much higher than a typical building of its type. Nevertheless, due to the nature of the building's use, they were a high priority. Several unique strategies were used to make the project feasible. The City of Chicago agreed to donate land to the organization because of the work it does for citizens with disabilities. An obsolete police station was being demolished on a very desirable site for private development. So the city gave Access Living half of the site and sold the other half to a private developer for a high-rise building. All three parties were winners. The city received enough revenue from the sale to the developer that it could afford to give the land to Access Living. The developer received a very rare commodity, a well-located site in downtown Chicago. They also had the city government behind them in approving their building proposal. Access Living received free land and a great location for serving the community. With city support, the fund-raising program for the project proved successful and all the aforementioned features were possible to include.

Operating budget

Inclusive design can lower operating costs dramatically, although the impact will depend on the type of building. There are several ways that cost savings might be realized. First, by increasing independence, the need for assistance by employees can be reduced. Second, improved safety can reduce accidents to employees and visitors and the cost of related legal claims. Even when a claim may be fraudulent, the overt practice of inclusive design demonstrates that the building owner and designers were using a higher than usual "standard of care." An example is the use of heated pavement at the entry to a building located in a cold region. By ensuring that ice and snow will never accumulate, the chances of slips and falls occurring due to maintenance lapses are practically eliminated. A good safety record can also reduce insurance premiums. Third, equipment and materials that are easy to use and maintain reduces the effort required by physical plant staff. Easy to use and understand equipment can also reduce damage due to improper use and resultant repair costs. Cleaning some waterless urinals, for example, requires the use of special cleansers and tools. If such urinals can be cleaned with the same cleansers and equipment used for toilet fixtures, problems can be avoided.

The costs and benefits of inclusive design cannot be measured solely by studying the inclusive design features themselves. Its impact on other design goals needs to be measured as well. For example, in sustainable buildings, automated environmental control systems are often used to control energy usage. Local thermostats are provided, but give only limited ranges of adjustments. This centralized approach to control requires a high-quality sensor and control system that allows building managers to understand and adjust settings for individual spaces where there are problems with thermal comfort due to microclimate effects, different levels of activity, or chronic health issues. If a good control system is not provided, frustrated occupants will open their windows during hot weather if it is too cold inside and during cold weather if it is too hot inside. They may also bring in their own space heaters to keep work spaces warm if it is too cold. At the worst, they will not work in their office, essentially abandoning the building, which could reduce communications with co-workers and productivity. Improper use of the building also can lead to serious maintenance and safety issues, such as excess humidity accumulating on surfaces. To reap the true economic benefits of inclusive design, it is best practiced in all realms of design, rather than considered as a separate package of features.

Life cycle costing

The cost of inclusive design is best understood from a life cycle cost perspective. The costs of construction are actually a very small part of the total cost of a building, once the operating costs over the life span of the building are computed. The life cycle perspective is used to justify higher first costs for sustainable building design, and it is also valid for inclusive design, but the cost savings are much harder to quantify. Unfortunately, no research has been completed yet on this topic and there are few examples from practice.

There are several life cycle benefits of inclusive design. The first is making buildings desirable to visit more than once. Designers like to believe that a strong aesthetic statement will attract people to a building and make them want to come back, but there is no evidence to demonstrate that this belief is valid. While an exciting building, from an aesthetic perspective, can attract visitors, a poor experience in the building can drive them away and ensure that they will never return. Inclusive design, on the other hand, may not attract people, but after visitors have a good experience in the building, they are more likely to return. Thus, one life cycle argument for inclusive design is retaining valued customers, clients, visitors, patients, and employees. The Kaiser supermarket chain in Germany reported a 30% increase in revenue when it incorporated inclusive design features in its stores.[7]

Another life cycle argument is increasing productivity of employees. Healthy buildings reduce illness and absenteeism, a major cost to employers. Buildings that support the tasks of employees help to increase productivity. Satisfied employees are more productive employees. Research on the impact of workplace design on employee satisfaction shows that the long-term benefits in productivity are significant compared with the first costs of construction.[8]

Cost-benefit analysis

Given the potential impact of inclusive design on operating costs, it is important to conduct at least a rudimentary cost-benefit analysis on features that may seem to be prohibitive in cost, before dismissing them out of hand. If the benefit of a feature affects the bottom line of an organization in an appreciable way by increasing revenue or reducing operating costs, then there is a good argument for putting a high priority on it. Sometimes the benefits are surprising. For example, the United Kingdom's Public Health Service studied the costs and benefits of single hospital rooms compared with double or multi-person rooms. A major operating cost for hospitals is the cost of treating infections patients acquire when they visit a hospital for other reasons. The research found that the increased capital cost for constructing a hospital with single rooms can be recouped only in three to five years "at the very most in a very conservative scenario."[9]

In a cost-benefit analysis, it is important to avoid exaggerating the initial cost. For example, the cost of an automated door needs to be adjusted by subtracting the cost of the alternative manual door. It is also important to estimate the true benefits, not just the most obvious ones. For example, a company developed a new technology for heating pavement. They installed it in an elevated transit platform in a Midwestern city to assess the economic impact of their product. They knew that with the heated pavement, no snow removal was required over the course of a winter. Typically, the platform had to be shoveled by a team of eight transit employees. The basic cost savings per year was the number of times shoveling was needed multiplied by the hourly wage of the workers multiplied by eight. However, in their investigation, they learned that the agency also used salt to melt ice and snow, therefore, the cost of the salt and the labor to spread it had to be added to the base cost. Further, the salt deteriorated the pavement, resulting in repair costs and reduction of its useful life. In addition, snow melting chemicals have a negative impact on the environment, resulting in a cost to society as well. Thus, there is a social capital investment for installing heated pavement. It is important to note, though, that every situation is different. For example, unionized employees of a transit agency make higher wages than non-union workers at a hotel, and a city with fewer freezing days with precipitation will probably not benefit as much from the same snow melting system.

Continual improvement budget

One of the most neglected budget factors is planning for continual improvement. Owners of buildings seem to think that once their new building is completed, all their facility-related problems will be solved. Typically, though, it is just the old, known problems that have been fixed. Once the new building is constructed, problems that were not perceived to be problems before suddenly become serious. The aforementioned air conditioning example is a good illustration of this phenomenon. Prior to renovation, if a building has no air conditioning, no one will complain that the temperature is too cold during hot weather.

The introduction of innovative ideas can result in unanticipated consequences. For example, cubicle farms and "open offices" were introduced to increase communication among members of work teams. The idea was this would increase productivity by reducing errors and delays in communications between members, as well as lead to synergy through increased informal contact. But research shows there is no increase in learning through informal interactions among workers in open work spaces versus workers in enclosed work spaces. Productivity of open office workers who need to concentrate is actually adversely affected by the lack of privacy and increased background noise. If innovative features with potentially serious consequences are incorporated in a building, it would be a good idea to have a Plan B with a budget to support it in case the experiment is flawed and renovations are needed. In open plan offices, for example, money for upgrading acoustics or the provision of some enclosed work spaces where workers can retreat to concentrate would be a good alternative if things do not work out as planned.[10]

Not only are there continuing needs for improvements related to unknown issues or unintended consequences, they can also be caused by social processes impacting the inhabitants of buildings over time. The most obvious is the aging of the population. A housing project that attracts "empty nesters" will be a project that houses elders in about 20 years. Some of their needs can be anticipated by the original building design, but others will only emerge over time. A neighborhood restaurant that is popular with families may find that over time, it loses its popularity as residents of the neighborhood age and high noise levels make it impossible for the regular clientele to converse comfortably.

Every building will need improvements after it is constructed. Most organizations have an annual budget for building maintenance and repairs, but they do not always have a budget for making improvements related to usability, safety, health, and social issues. Establishing such a budget will help to reap the long-term benefits of an inclusively designed building. Even a small budget can be beneficial because it can be put aside until enough is available to address an important need in future years.

Dwelling on the cost of inclusive design features diverts attention from the overall economic argument for any building feature. Including only the lowest cost solutions to any design project rarely leads to a decent result. Even with minimum budgets, priorities need to be made to ensure that the most important goals of a project are met. If they can't, one has to question the feasibility of the project. Further, the social capital, life cycle costs, and benefits of a feature need to be assessed before making decisions. False choices need to be exposed and understood. Sometimes, like the example of single rooms in hospitals, a very costly feature can reap significant economic benefits, more than paying for itself over time. The real argument is about value. How important is a feature to the mission of the organization? Will it help to reduce or contain operating costs? What is the long-term net cost or benefit? What is the social capital that will result from investment? These are the questions that need to be asked. In the design process, advocates of inclusive design need to be prepared for the inevitable cost argument with arguments about value. And, ideally, they should be able to support their positions with good evidence. Over time, research and practice will identify the costs and benefits of inclusive design and help to provide an evidence base for practice, but this requires many more buildings to be constructed with inclusive design features.

Notes

1 Steinfeld, Edward, Jordana Maisel, David Feathers, and Clive D'Souza. "Anthropometry and Standards for Wheeled Mobility: An International Comparison." *Assistive Technology* 22.1 (2010): 51–67.

2 Mid-Ohio Regional Planning Commission. "Complete Streets Toolkit." MORPC, 2012. www.morpc.org/trans/CS_Toolkit_Web_Lo_Res.pdf.

3 Steinfeld, Edward, and Jonathan R. White. *Inclusive Housing: A Pattern Book: Design for Diversity and Equality*. New York: W. W. Norton & Company, Inc., 2010.

4 Fischel, W. "An Economic History of Zoning and a Cure for Its Exclusionary Effects." *Urban Studies* 41.2 (2004): 317–340; and Talen, Emily. *Design for Diversity*. Boston, MA: Elsevier Ltd., 2012.

5 Lynott, Jana, Jessica Haase, Kristin Nelson, Amanda Taylor, Hannah Twaddell, Jared Ulmer, Barbara McCann, and Edward R. Stollof. *Planning Complete Streets for an Aging America*. No. 2009–02, 2009; and McCann, Barbara, and Suzanne Rynne. *Complete Streets: Best Policy and Implementation Practices*. American Planning Association Report 559, 2010.

6 Schroeder, Steven, and Edward Steinfeld. *The Estimated Cost of Accessible Buildings*. Washington, DC: Dept. of Housing and Urban Development, Office of Policy Development and Research, 1979; and Steven Winter Associates, and United States Department of Housing and Urban Development. *Office of Policy Development and Research. Cost of Accessible Housing: An Analysis of the Estimated Cost of Compliance With the Fair Housing Accessibility Guidelines And ANSI A 117.1*. Washington, DC: The Office, 1993.

7 Steinfeld, Edward, and Jordana L. Maisel. *Universal Design: Creating Inclusive Environments*. Hoboken, NJ: John Wiley & Sons, Inc., 2012.

8 Weidemann, Sue, and CP&Associates. "Lewis & Clark State Office Building: Post Occupancy Evaluation." Final Report to the State of Missouri Office of Administrations, Division of Facilities Management Design & Construction, 179, 2008; and Brill, Michael, Sue Weidemann, and BOSTI Associates. *Disproving Widespread Myths About Workplace Design*. Jasper, IN: Kimball International, 2001.

9 Stall, Nathan. "Private Rooms: The Fiscal Advantage." *CMAJ: Canadian Medical Association Journal* 184.1 (2012): E47–E48; and Chaudhury, Habib, Atiya

Mahmood, and Maria Valente. *The Use of Single Patient Rooms vs. Multiple Occupancy Rooms in Acute Care Environments.* Simon Fraser University, Coalition for Health Environments Research, 2004.

10 Weidemann, Sue, and CP&Associates. "Lewis & Clark State Office Building: Post Occupancy Evaluation." Final Report to the State of Missouri Office of Administrations, Division of Facilities Management Design & Construction, 2008.

chapter 2

Design

On any given project, architects make thousands of decisions – some major, some minor; some pre-planned, some incremental, and others improvised. These decisions cut across an array of issues: structural limits, budgetary constraints, legal requirements, client goals, performance targets, and aesthetic aspirations. Many issues – and many stakeholders – can be viewed as possessing competing aims and interests, requiring the design and construction team to mediate these factors and often negotiate among themselves. One point of view on this complexity is to see inclusive design, much like sustainability or value engineering, as one more factor to consider. An alternative view, the one we are emphasizing, is that inclusive design is an overarching means of integrating, not competing with, other design factors. Designing from the perspective of human diversity provides a means to evaluate alternative strategies for site design, spatial organization and wayfinding, the design of individual spaces, and the selection of environmental controls and furnishings. Inclusive design provides a framework for making decisions that support the health, safety, productivity, enjoyment, and autonomy of a site and building's occupants.

How does inclusive design influence site design?

When designing sites, several factors contribute to the usability and functioning of the project, such as sensitivity to the social context, sympathy with the local ecology and natural environment, continuity of circulation and movement, and acuity regarding material selection. While manipulating topography, discussed shortly, is one of the first acts, and one of the finishing acts, in the construction of a building, inclusive site design originates with an understanding of the cultural context. Connecting to the surrounding built fabric, such as transportation systems and other buildings/ sites of significance, is one facet. Closely aligned is understanding patterns of daily life – where people live, work, play, eat, and so forth; at what times; and in what places – which, in turn, informs when and how people will likely arrive to and leave from the building and site being designed. Cultural norms also play a role. Are there important religious rituals? Are there beliefs regarding building and site orientation? Are there ideals of proportion, materials, or space making? What are the gender norms, and how are aging, disability, and other social constructs understood? The aim in answering these questions is to inform design decisions that reduce stigma and ensure safety, especially for the most vulnerable groups in the community in which the building resides.

Grading, water management, and landscape design

The topography of a landscape, a street, or a sidewalk, and the design of the transition to the building entry, can permit (or limit) access to the building across a range of user groups, particularly people with compromised strength, equilibrium, or stamina, such as older adults, small children, and individuals with acute injuries. Grading, or the manipulation of topography and landscapes, is a core task of site design, particularly for open-site buildings and complexes. The aims are twofold: (1) to effectively manage storm water and other surface waters and (2) to design meaningful building-landscape relationships. These two goals gain added importance through the inclusive design process.

Managing rainwater, as well as underground water flows and surface water bodies such as springs, wetlands, and streams, has been a critical concern of architects and builders since the beginning of civilization, as groundwater impacts the durability of a building, particularly the foundations. More recently, increased attention to design for resiliency has altered the way that topography is transformed and landscape materials are selected. In flood-prone areas, buildings are being raised above grade or designed so that living spaces are not located at grade levels. But both these strategies can introduce significant barriers to physical access, especially in places where the flood plain is quite high like in the Mississippi Delta or along seashores where hurricanes are common. A key inclusive design strategy in such locations is the incorporation of an accessible infrastructure that enables all sites to share expensive vertical circulation elements like ramps and public elevators. Traditional raised boardwalks are a good precedent of such infrastructure.

Increasing the ability of a site to reduce runoff to surrounding areas is another sustainability strategy. Permeable pavements let water seep through them and collect in groundwater or in underground collection areas. Permeable pavement materials include gravel, brick, cobblestones, permeable concrete pavement, porous asphalt, stabilized soils, and gravel. Unfortunately, these materials are also the most difficult for pedestrian travel and wheeled mobility device use. This does not mean that managing surface water and inclusive design are mutually exclusive goals. The consideration of both together leads to creative solutions like paving limited areas in the center or sides of pathways with smooth stable materials like traditional concrete and using porous materials on the rest (see Figure 2.1).

Topography often needs to be adjusted on a site to prepare it for building, but it is also one of the most important decisions regarding ease of access.

2.1 Pavers providing a track for wheeled mobility devices

When modifying site topography through grading, the following three issues need to be addressed:

1   Wayfinding: how can grading and landscape design assist people in understanding the organization of the site, paths of travel, destinations, and entries? Topography and landscape elements can be used to hide secondary or unintended paths and destinations while revealing primary ones, and materials can be used to clarify paths of movement, versus spaces of repose, versus areas not intended for occupancy. In complement, continuity of paths (spatially and materially) along with clear definition of thresholds and entries (again, through changes in materials and spatial definition) can dramatically improve wayfinding among people with visual and cognitive impairments. Acoustic elements, such as fountains or foliage, can enhance the sensory experience and provide additional wayfinding cues.

2   Ease of movement: how can grading and landscape design provide a steady and seamless path of travel? Careful manipulation of topography can ease movement for people using an array of personal modes of transit – from walkers to wheelchairs, bicycles to powered scooters – as well as children, older adults, and people with health conditions that might minimize stamina. Even steep sites and longer paths of travel can become manageable through the creative integration of areas for rest and/or the use of the building and its circulation systems to negotiate changes in elevation.

3   Safety and comfort: how can grading and landscape design improve user comfort, particularly in relation to sun, rain, and wind? Poor management of surface water, for example, can result in slippery, sometimes impassible, areas on exterior paths. By contrast, a well-designed site will help to mitigate extreme heat and cold, as well as wind, humidity, and rain. Again, this concerns the safety and comfort of all users, but is especially important for children, the frail elderly, and people who face difficulty in self-regulating body temperature. Strategies for improving human comfort in the exterior environment, such as planting shade trees or providing windbreaks, can be integrated with wayfinding and other strategies to improve the user experience in both domains (wayfinding and comfort).

2.2 Walkway system connecting two levels on the J. Paul Getty Museum Campus in Los Angeles, California

Suburban and urban development in hilly areas has, for too long, treated steep topography as a territory to be conquered using methods like flattening the hills to build big-box stores and large parking lots. In sustainable development, designers seek to work with the topography. Steep sites are not inherently inaccessible. By planning natural terracing and pathways that use their length to overcome slope differences, natural contours can be maintained and manipulation of topography is less drastic. Elevators in buildings can be used to connect upper and lower levels of sites, and access to buildings can be at mid-floor or top-floor locations rather than bottom floors. Using the natural slope of a site to support access is not only more sustainable than grading sites to be level; it can, if planned well, enhance accessibility of a site for everyone (see Figure 2.2.).

Responding to weather, ecology, and other contextual factors

Noted as early as the first century BCE in Vitruvius' *Ten Books on Architecture*, site selection and design impact well-being. Weather, ecology, and the surrounding built environment especially influence air quality, which, in turn, influences human health. In a growing number of cities and regions throughout the world, buildings must account for outdoor air pollution, natural allergens, and fluctuations in weather that affect indoor air quality. Commensurately, each site design possesses its own microclimate and ecology, which can add to or diminish other health risks. Standing water, for example, can enable mosquito breeding and, thereby, exacerbate the spread of mosquito-borne diseases like malaria, West Nile virus, dengue, yellow fever, and Zika virus. Some plants, like birch trees, produce high levels of allergens in their pollen that can contribute to increased seasonal allergy symptoms.

Integrating modes of transit

A primary goal that underpins all site design is the integration of various modes of human movement, both locomotion and transportation. This begins with an understanding of how people arrive at the site, for example, on foot, bus, train, car, bicycle, and so forth. People in dense, urban areas, as well as those who live in, work on, or visit large-scale complexes like college campuses, often rely on multiple modes of transportation. As each mode is often

2.3 Evacuation of nursing home patients amid Hurricane Katrina in New Orleans, Louisiana
Photo by FEMA/Jocelyn Augustino

designed, maintained, and managed by a different agency or office, the connectivity between systems can be poorly considered. To improve convenience and functionality, the design team needs to consider transportation systems from the users' perspectives and how transitions are made from one mode of transit to another, for example, car to wheelchair, bus to a bike, and how to accommodate the time spent waiting for rides. Design must also consider the continuum from site access to building entry, and all transitions that occur along the way. A failure at any link in the system can unintentionally terminate access, especially for people with mobility impairments. Increasingly, we must also consider how emergency access and evacuation of sites will take place. The most vulnerable populations, like people with disabilities, frail older people, people who are health care patients, and those with low incomes, are, unfortunately, often the last to be evacuated because they are physically unable to respond independently or have no access to private transportation (see Figure 2.3).

How does inclusive design promote convenience and wayfinding inside the building?

Wayfinding is the organization and communication of our dynamic relationship to space and the environment. Successful wayfinding design allows people to: (1) determine their location within a setting, (2) determine their destination, and (3) develop a plan that will take them from their location to their destination. The design of wayfinding systems need to include: (1) identifying and marking spaces, (2) grouping spaces, and (3) linking and organizing spaces through both architectural and graphic means. All strategies used for wayfinding must communicate effectively to the broadest group possible, including people with a wide range of sensory abilities, intellectual abilities, literacy levels, languages, and physical statures. Design for good wayfinding is even more critical when movement through a building must occur under great time constraints, such as evacuation during an emergency.

Spatial organization

Certain architectural and interior design features help users to construct a mental map of a place by creating familiar models of how space is organized, by supporting multisensory access to information, and distinguishing one place from another. There are five attributes of buildings and sites that support the construction of accurate mental maps: (1) clearly defined paths and circulation systems, (2) markers that stand out from the general background stimuli, (3) recognizable nodes where paths intersect, (4) strong edges such as walls or landscape features, and (5) well-defined zones/districts.

Strategy 2.1   Circulation systems

When designing circulation systems, utilize five complementary spatial elements: paths, markers, nodes, edges, and zones.

Paths

The circulation system is the key organizing element of a site or building. Designing an inclusive circulation system includes the following guidelines:

- Communicate the circulation system to the users when they enter. In particular, vertical circulation devices, such as ramps, stairs, escalators, lifts, and elevators, need to be intuitive and perceptible (see Figure 2.4).
- Develop a focal point and a system of circulation paths to help people understand where they are in the system.
- Distinguish paths with width/height, material, and color differences to assist in the comprehension of the circulation system.
- Use a system that has repetition or rhythm to help people determine intuitively where they are going and be able to anticipate destinations.
- Use circulation systems that lead people from node to node (see Figure 2.5).
- In multistory buildings, organize elements such as restrooms, elevators, and exits in the same location on each floor. Remember that people often do not comprehend the overall plan of circulation paths. Whenever possible, design layouts that enable people to identify where they are going well before they arrive.
- Where possible, emergency circulation routes should be the same as those used for regular building functions. Where separate emergency circulation routes are needed, they must be visible to building users during normal use of the building.

2.4 Options for vertical movement within a building

2.5 Tactile floor leading to information desk

Markers

Markers such as arches, monuments, building entrances, kiosks, banners, artwork, and natural features give strong identities to various parts of a site or building (see Figure 2.6). They act as mental landmarks in the wayfinding process and break a complex task into manageable parts. Inclusive guidelines to consider include the following:

■ Place markers at focal points that correspond to intersections.
■ Locate markers to be detectable from as many positions as possible without physically interrupting the path of travel.
■ In interiors, consider hanging markers.
■ Mark entrances by adding cues such as recesses, overhangs, and/or landscaping.
■ When designing building exit markers, equate light cues with exit conditions.
■ Set up primary markers to incorporate tactile, sound, and visual indicators.

2.6 Wayfinding in Stuttgart City Library by Yi Architects. The Stuttgart City Library by Yi Architects is a wayfinding exemplar. Overall circulation is visible from all levels. Each floor contains a multisensory directory. The center is lit by an oculus skylight that emphasizes the square marker below.

- Locate windows to enable detection of markers from inside.
- Establish unique views to the outdoors as interior markers.
- Consider the information desk or kiosk to be a key wayfinding marker.
- Use unique markers to identify emergency circulation systems if they are separate from the normal circulation system.

Nodes

Nodes are places where paths come together. People make decisions at nodes in paths. As a result, nodes might contain graphic and architectural information to assist with those decisions. Inclusive guidelines to consider include the following:

- Distinguish nodes with markers and general architectural features.
- Think of wayfinding as a "connect-the-dots" activity and use only the information that is necessary at each node.
- Consider easy-to-understand node systems such as grids to help people establish a mental map of the wayfinding system.
- Use maps and graphic information to communicate the form of circulation only at primary rather than secondary nodes.
- Make certain that the level of information provided at nodes is not overwhelming, especially for first-time visitors who need to access essential information for finding their way.

Edges

Edges such as walls, handrails, floor strips, and planter rows provide a physical means to orient oneself in space. An edge provides a boundary that people use to move in the right direction. Inclusive guidelines to consider include the following:

- Design edges for both visual and tactile detection.
- Change edge features periodically to provide a sense of progress toward a goal as one is moving along.
- Introduce contrasting floor textures and hardness to establish wayfinding edge conditions and to alert users to changes in height conditions.
- Mark the tops and bottoms of ramps and stairs to emphasize transition points.
- Use tactile marking systems on handrails to inform people of changes in conditions, particularly potentially hazardous conditions (e.g., the top step of a stairway).

Zones

Wayfinding zones are regions either outside or within buildings with a distinguishing character that assist in the general identification of place. Inclusive guidelines to consider when designing wayfinding zones include the following:

- Establish zones at the beginning of the design process.
- Identify each zone as memorable and unique from the other zones.
- Use unifying elements such as a tactile pattern, color, sound, themed images, or even hypoallergenic scent (see Figure 2.7).
- Reinforce the identifying characteristics of the zone with signage prior to arrival in the zone.
- Identify zones with names such as the North Wing or Green Grass South.

2.7 Wayfinding system in medical office. Pictorial cues at multiple scales help all find their way and are particularly beneficial to those with language and memory challenges. At this medical facility, patients are given an image and are instructed to follow the image to find their way to the specialty area.

2.7 Continued

How does inclusive design affect environmental controls?

Intrinsic to the definition of inclusive design is the promotion of human performance, health, and well-being. Environmental controls, such as lighting and HVAC systems, affect the ways that users interact with their surrounding environments. Over the past decade, the sustainability movement has increased its focus on the promotion of human health in addition to the health of the earth. This shared relationship between inclusive design and sustainability continues to strengthen as researchers strive to demonstrate that efforts supporting the health of the environment also support human health. While environmental controls are able to support human functioning in the built environment, they are also capable, if not planned, designed, and installed correctly, of acting as barriers. When designing through an inclusive lens, it is essential to properly select and implement environmental control systems appropriate for the users and function of the space. This section describes the role that lighting and HVAC systems play in promoting human performance and health and wellness.

Lighting

Lighting influences a variety of human factors including task performance, spatial appearance, safety and security, and mental health. While studies repeatedly show proper lighting levels contribute to increased human performance and comfort in a space, recent research in the field of photobiology suggests it also has effects on human circadian rhythms. As a result, both electric and daylighting are necessary elements.[1]

Electric lighting comes in several forms, including the incandescent bulb, halogen lamp, gaseous discharge varieties (e.g., metal halide, fluorescent tubes, compact fluorescents), and light-emitting diode (LED) (see Figure 2.8). No matter the form, electric lighting is most beneficial when provided in a manner in which it is continuous and even. To accommodate the wide range of tasks performed in spaces like offices and kitchens, designers need to provide general, ambient, and task lighting with controls for each type, allowing users to manage the amount and type of light needed for

2.8 LED lighting in retail setting

2.9 General, ambient, and task lighting in kitchen

particular tasks (see Figure 2.9). Positioning fixtures so light is indirect, or otherwise diffused, helps to minimize distracting glare and/or shadows that may contribute to human discomfort, error, fatigue, or injury.

Strategy 2.2   Lighting

To improve human comfort and performance, it is best to provide day-lighting and electric lighting, whether independent or in combination, in a continuous, even, and indirect manner, while also enabling user control over the amount and directionality of lighting in critical task areas.

To avoid negative effects on visual perception and comfort when users move from one room to another, such as from assembly spaces to corridors, optimally, light-level changes occur gradually between spaces. Additionally, in dimly lit areas, including performance spaces, designers can use electric lighting or photo-luminescent materials to define path edges. In large spaces with multiple users, for example, open office environments, the design optimally provides task lighting with individual controls to facilitate user control over the amount of light based on individual needs. Emergency circulation routes must be easily perceived when the building loses electrical power and emergency lighting is functioning at lower levels of illumination than normal lighting.

With multiple light sources, though, it is sometimes difficult to avoid having too much light or poor quality of light in a space. Likewise, efficient lighting control is an important aspect of both sustainable and inclusive design. Controls that automatically adjust electric lighting levels based on the amount of daylight available, as well as presence-detection systems, increase usability and promote sustainability. While fine adjustments by users may still be required, automation can reduce the frequency of interventions. It is important that automated systems are understandable to the users and are compatible with their habits. Sometimes manual systems can accomplish the same goals with less cost and greater control. For example, hotels often incorporate a master switch that the guest's card key activates. This may be a better approach to shutting off lights in a hotel room than a presence sensor, since there is relatively little activity in such spaces and lights will automatically turn off even though there may be people in the room. New remote systems that can be operated by smartphones offer greater potential for personalized control over lighting, both natural and artificial.[2]

Even with proper planning and design of illumination, without adequate lighting controls, the most efficient artificial lighting system can become inadequate to meet the needs of users. To ensure the most effective use of artificial lighting, utilize the following strategies:

- Lighting controls that are within reach;
- Lighting controls that are labeled to indicate their zone of control;
- Switch plates that contrast in color from the surrounding wall;
- Lighting controls that can be activated by remote control or voice command;
- Automated lighting that also includes an override switch; and
- Lighting controls that have a master switch to control all light.

Case study 2.1 – big-box stores

Historically, time zones and daylight hours set the parameters of business hours for many offices and commercial establishments. With the emergence of chain stores across vast geographies, headquarters centrally monitor and control the lighting and other systems in their big-box stores, turning the lights off shortly after the stores close and on shortly before the stores open. Striving for efficiency, unintended consequences arose. One such consequence related to central managers setting national systems based on local parameters. As a result, franchises with southern headquarters heard from managers of stores in far northern locations who found that employees were arriving to pitch black parking lots early in the morning. To ensure safety of their personnel, they had to break into locked control boxes in their stores and disconnect automated systems. In this case, the problem is not due to the control system itself, but to the limitations of its software and the nearsightedness of its operators. A system like this has to be more sophisticated to address the different contextual conditions of hundreds or thousands of stores, including an understanding that the length of day and night varies not only by time zone, but, also by latitude, as well as daily weather.

As is the case for electric lighting, it is important to provide access to daylight in all habitable spaces. The provision of natural light in a space can be accomplished using two types of systems: side-lighting systems and top-lighting systems. Side-lighting systems provide lateral illumination from the sides of the building, while top-lighting systems provide vertical illumination from the top of the building. Unlike artificial lighting, which is easily controlled by switches and/or knobs, natural lighting is somewhat more difficult to manage because it requires the management of not only the quantity of light, but also the quality. Sidelight systems accomplish this by utilizing features such as light shelves, prismatic glazing, mirrors and/or holograms, anidolic ceilings, and louvers and/or blinds. Top-light systems control the amount and quality of light through skylights, roof monitors, saw-tooth systems, or light pipe systems (see Figure 2.10). One key

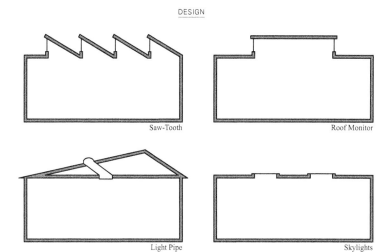

Saw-Tooth

Roof Monitor

Light Pipe

Skylights

2.10 Top-lighting strategies

challenge posed by daylight is that it changes based on the time of day and time of year. In order to lessen the reliance on users to account for these gradual changes, technologies such as shading devices that automatically adjust based on the amount of natural light available and/or time of day/ year can be incorporated into the design. This not only will help to ensure occupant comfort but also will lessen the additional load placed on other systems.[3]

HVAC systems

HVAC systems have the ability to affect user comfort and contribute to health promotion and avoidance of disease as well. In studies examining workplace satisfaction, experts cite thermal comfort – the condition of mind that expresses satisfaction with the thermal environment, assessed by subjective evaluation – as the number one complaint of workers. To address this, there are many strategies designers can adopt to ensure user comfort, including specifying HVAC systems that are engineered to provide even and stable temperatures within a zone. This is supported by paying special attention to placement of heating coils, diffusers, and exhaust elements, and also insulation levels in walls, doors, and windows.

Strategy 2.3   HVAC systems

As the leading complaint among employees is thermal comfort, and, as thermal comfort is subjective and highly varied, HVAC systems must be flexible in accommodating an array of user needs and preferences.

In environments such as office buildings, zoning systems allow for the independent control of spaces, facilitating comfort for a wide variety of users at different times of the day. Another option is to include supplemental heating and cooling units in individual task areas. This can assist with maintaining thermal comfort in spaces that may experience significant fluctuations in temperature throughout the day because of their location on certain exposures of the building, for example, north facing vs. south facing, or use of different equipment. Supplemental systems allow for adjustments to easily be made within a space without affecting the comfort of occupants in other parts of the building.[4]

While the type of system provided has the ability to affect user comfort, the design of the system itself can greatly affect occupant health. Ideally, architects and engineers design HVAC systems to: (1) eliminate drafts by design or through controls on airflow, (2) incorporate high-efficiency air filters and allergen filtering systems, and (3) allow for natural ventilation options. Research shows that proper airflow, ventilation, and air quality contribute to increased productivity and reduced incidence of illness.[5]

To maximize system effectiveness, appropriate attention must be paid to implementation. System controls must be reachable by all people and follow a common user interface. While an HVAC system may be designed to achieve the highest level of efficiency, if the controls are not intuitive, accessible, and easy to use, the system will never be used in such a way to achieve this efficiency.

How does inclusive design affect the design of key features?

Parking

Parking is often the first element of a site user's experience when arriving at a building or public space. Accessibility codes specify minimum requirements for parking, including a specified number of reserved spaces for people with disabilities as well as access aisles to facilitate transfer into and out of vehicles. Codes do not, however, address the parking needs of other segments of the population, including pregnant women, older people, families with small children, and incentive programs, such as employee-of-the-month initiatives. In addition, owners often provide spaces reserved for people who pay a fee for greater convenience or with electrical supply for charging electric vehicles as an incentive to promote the purchase of electric or hybrid vehicles, and to encourage ride-sharing. In response to these needs, the term "priority parking" is used here to describe the inclusion of spaces for these groups. Priority parking is most effective when it is located close to main entrances to buildings or public spaces. It may be appropriate that any fees associated with priority parking be waived for people with disabilities. It is important that any type of priority parking that provides unique benefits or services, for example, EV charging stations, include accessible parking spaces as well.

Strategy 2.4   Priority parking

Rather than a binary approach to parking design – that is, design for "handicapped" and general-use parking – consider parking as a spectrum of options for diverse occupants. Proximity to the destination is but one feature in "priority parking." Other features, such as shade, protected walking paths, lighting, and amenities like charging stations, can be deployed to better meet the needs and preferences of various user groups, and incentivize otherwise underused parking areas.

Paving and walkways

The design and construction of walking surfaces is critically important to the safety of users when navigating any site. For public rights-of-way, accessibility codes and standards provide extensive guidance on design for people with disabilities by specifying requirements, for example, ensuring walking surfaces are stable, firm, and slip resistant, and free of objects protruding into the path of travel. Also dictated are maximum running slopes in the direction of travel and cross slopes perpendicular to the path of travel, as well as minimum widths for pathways, typically based on the space needed for one wheelchair user. When approaching paving and walkways through an inclusive lens, the design may include higher-level strategies that address usability, safety, and security on all paths and walkways, not just those addressed by accessibility code requirements. These strategies may include the following:

- Site-related considerations, such as the provision of finished topography that diverts water from pathways;
- Material considerations including the use of permeable pavement to aid in reducing the collection of water on surfaces;
- Material changes signifying pathway and/or walkway edge conditions;
- Lighting to illuminate walking surfaces; and
- Reflective or photo-luminescent materials to mark edge conditions at night.[6]

The ability to detect the edges between pedestrian and vehicular areas is critical to the safety not only of users with visual impairment but also to other users. This can be accomplished by using cobblestone or brick-lined edges, plantings, bollards, spheres, or even guardrails. Designing beyond the minimum regulated standards for individual features also improves usability and functionality for all users. For instance, designing the width of a sidewalk based on the expected capacity rather than the minimum space required for wheelchair use ensures users with and without disabilities are able to comfortably navigate. Moreover, additional width provides an opportunity to include plantings, signage, and furniture to improve aesthetics, support usability, and accommodate user needs.

Case study 2.2 – Botanical Garden, Naples, Florida

The Botanical Garden in Naples, Florida, has a far-flung network of paths and also a large number of older visitors who have difficulty walking. The Garden provides scooters and wheelchairs for visitors who cannot manage the long distances required to see all the facilities. The buildings on-site are concentrated at the entry pavilion where the mobility devices can be checked out. The pavilion and other buildings with a dining area, gift store, offices, and auditorium are raised above grade to protect them against flooding (see Figure 2.11). A continuous deck and bridges connect them all with an accessible circulation

2.11 Raised walkway system at Naples Botanical Garden, Naples, Florida

2.12 Protected walkway at Naples Botanical Garden in Naples, Florida

path with ramped access from grade. All circulation areas are wider than the minimum to accommodate both the mobility devices and large crowds. The bridges, ramps, and decks are also covered to protect them during rainy periods (see Figure 2.12).

Ramps

Ramps are an inclusive solution to navigating changes in elevation where stairs would typically be used. Accessibility standards set forth several requirements for the design of ramps including:

- Maximum width
- Maximum length
- Maximum slope
- Railing design
- Edge protection
- Landing design.

Although these requirements begin to address usability and safety for users with disabilities, research shows that these measures are often inadequate to address the needs of many users with and without disabilities. Ramps designed to the maximum slope and length often incite fatigue among manual wheeled mobility device users and their caregivers, and minimum landing sizes are often inadequate to accommodate the turning space needed for larger wheeled mobility devices and even strollers. Additionally, ramps are often implemented as an alternative path of travel to stairs, typically requiring a longer path of travel located outside the main pedestrian path.

Inclusively designed ramps often include programming strategies, such as incorporating a ramp as the main path running in the direction of primary circulation, assisting in reduction of user effort (see Figure 2.13). Reducing the slope below the maximum allowed also helps to minimize user effort. The ramp design must also take into account the expected traffic and largest wheeled mobility device users when specifying the width of ramp runs and dimensions of the landing. Additionally, the inclusion of seating along

2.13 Boardwalk at Cape Cod National Seashore in Provincetown, Massachusetts

the ramp or landings not only benefits users who may fatigue easily or have limited mobility but also provides a space for users to get out of the way while waiting for someone or who may need to stop for any reason, such as to make a phone call.

Strategy 2.5 Ramp design

Rather than a secondary feature, inclusive design practices often position features, such as ramps, as signature building elements – central to the overriding architectural concept and user experience.

Stairs

In places and spaces where a change in elevation deems it necessary to have stairs, approaching stair design in a thoughtful way can make them more usable for a wider population of users. Existing accessibility regulations apply only to stairs that are part of a means of egress and, at that, specify only the following features:

- Riser height
- Tread and nosing depth
- Tread surface
- Railing design
- Minimum landing sizes.

To make all stairs safer and more usable by people of all abilities, architects can pursue a number of inclusive strategies, including features that support situational awareness for everyone, especially individuals with sensory impairments. These features may include the following:

- Tactile warning-surface indicators at the top of stair runs;
- Tactile and/or auditory cues to indicate changes of direction and the top and bottom of a stair run (see Figure 2.14);

2.14 Cues at transitional moments on stairs in the House of Disabled People's Organisations in Taastrup, Denmark

- Riser and tread proportions that support a comfortable gait;
- Slip-resistant materials on treads; and
- The avoidance of irregularities onto the tread surface that can present tripping hazards.

The visual environment of the stairway is a critical factor in stair safety and usability. Strategies for creating a good visual environment include the following:

- Illuminating stair treads and handrails evenly;
- Using materials that reduce glare;
- Utilizing contrasting colors at the edges and handrails/balustrades to emphasize direction changes;
- Providing a contrasting color to emphasize the edge of stair nosings;
- Deploying non-distracting or non-confusing colors;
- Avoiding the use of textures and patterns on treads and landings that camouflage the edge of the stair treads or that create optical illusions;
- Controlling artificial and natural light to eliminate strong shadows on stair treads; and
- Including reflective or photo-luminescent striping in dark locations.

In addition to the design of stair risers and treads, design features on the landing also support usability. Similar to ramps, going beyond the minimum and including extra space on the landing provides not only an area for users to rest out of the flow of circulation, but also space for the inclusion of seating.

Strategy 2.6   Complementary features

While stairs and ramps are primarily designed as spaces of movement, consider how complementary elements, such as seating, can enhance the user experience. The concept of "complementary design" can be applied to all types of interior and exterior spaces.

Residential entries

No-step access into a home is one way to make a home more usable for people of all abilities. A no-step entry, or a flush entry, from the outside or garage, into the home is equally beneficial to someone with a mobility impairment as it is to a parent pushing a stroller or someone rolling a piece of luggage. No-step entries can be achieved using the following strategies:

- Slab-on-grade or notched foundations;
- Ramps to at least one entrance, including inside attached garages if space permits (see Figure 2.15); and
- Sloped walkways and careful grading of the site to eliminate the need for ramps.

Materials commonly used in the construction of residential ramps include wood, concrete, or composite decking. An alternative means to achieve a no-step entry is to include a platform lift. While not viewed as

2.15 Ramp to entrance of home

attractive as a well-designed ramp, platform lifts require significantly less space than a ramp and may also be incorporated into the entry sequence at any entrance to the home, including in a garage or mudroom, when space and headroom allows. One potential negative to platform lifts is the potential for mechanical failure.

While ramps and platform lifts provide solutions to achieve a no-step entry, both also carry a certain level of stigma and are often associated with disability. In keeping with this, an alternative solution is to construct the entry so it can be accessed from a grade or a sloping walkway – a walkway with a slope of 1:20 or less that requires no handrail (see Figure 2.16). A number of strategies can be used to achieve this condition including a reverse brick ledge foundation. To prevent water infiltration, a no-step entry using this method needs to include both a roof overhang and good outside drainage.

Building regulations do not always require accessibility to balconies, terraces, and decks. They often only require one accessible entry/exit. But

2.16 Sloping residential entry path in home show house by Heartland Homes

to participate fully in the life of a household, these outdoor spaces must be accessible – an essential principle of inclusive design in housing. To simplify construction, balconies, decks, and terraces are often designed to be one step below the interior floor level of the dwelling units they serve. The step is provided to prevent wind-driven water from entering the dwelling, prevent moisture from exterior build-up of ice and snow, or to reduce the complexity of the construction detail where the outside floor structure attaches to the building structure. For example, if an on-grade terrace is a poured-in-place slab, lowering it below the interior floor level eliminates the need to ensure the seam between the two structures is perfectly aligned; or, a concrete balcony will be lowered one step and sloped away from the building as an economical way to drain storm water away from the building wall. There is no reason why these spaces, with proper detailing, cannot be made accessible. If the entry utilizes a patio door, slotted decking and flashing can be used to limit the transference of water from outside to inside.[7]

Kitchen workstations and adjustable cabinetry

The inclusion of varied height workstations and adjustable cabinetry in kitchens and bathrooms increases convenience and helps to reduce effort for users of all abilities. Ideally, several counter height options between 28–42 in (715–1070 mm) will accommodate the needs of most users. Countertops at sinks are typically set at 36 in (915 mm) high, and standing workstations for reading and writing typically are best at 42 in (1070 mm). A counter height of 28–32 in (715–815 mm) satisfies the needs of most users when in a seated position. Raising ovens and dishwashers off the floor also reduces effort while cooking and loading dishes (see Figure 2.17).

Adaptable cabinetry is another option to ensure that the needs of diverse users are met. Adaptable cabinetry allows a kitchen or bathroom to be adjusted over time to meet changing occupant needs and preferences. Features like removable cabinet fronts on bases under sinks and workstations can provide knee clearance for someone who needs to sit or make use of a wheeled mobility device while completing tasks. Similarly, modular, stacking drawer units can be used to allow the height of a detachable countertop to be lowered or raised based on the needs and preferences of different users.

2.17 Raised dishwasher in home show house by Heartland Homes

Strategy 2.7 Adaptable kitchens

Kitchens are high-activity areas with diverse users. Designing with adaptability in mind can help accommodate small children and adults, as well as ambulatory and non-ambulatory residents over the life of a home. Adjustable cabinetry, along with work surfaces of various heights, extends the range of usability (see Figure 2.18).

Adjustable cabinetry is a challenge to implement despite the widespread adoption of adjustable storage systems like closet organizers. Kitchen cabinet and plumbing fixture manufacturers in Europe and North America have developed adjustable products, but they are hard to find and often expensive.

2.18 Inclusive residential kitchen

In some countries, the concept of adaptable cabinetry has been included as an option in accessibility codes for multifamily housing. The idea is to design cabinets so that minimal effort is needed to adapt the cabinets to wheelchair access by removing base cabinets and lowering counters. Adaptable cabinetry provides a bonus to the building developer and owner because less space is needed in small rooms to provide wheelchair turning clearances when the cabinets are removed under counters and plumbing fixtures. But it is still not widely used, partly because legacy codes still require a specified number of "adapted" units with knee clearances and lower counter and cabinet heights. This code provision is perceived as the answer to the problem of inaccessible cabinetry. However, having countertops and storage that is adaptable to an individual's needs is a universal need, not something from which only wheelchair users can benefit. For example, people of shorter stature and taller stature are uncomfortable and at risk of injury if work surfaces are not at heights that are appropriate for them. Retrieving objects out of reach can expose people to risks of falling or back injury.

Adaptable cabinetry can have many features:

- Adjustable shelving;
- Full-height pantry storage that provides options for people of different statures;
- Multiple-height work surfaces;
- Counters that can be repositioned to desirable heights for a household without a specialist;
- Automated countertops and cabinets that work for people seated and tall people standing;
- Storage on the back of cabinet doors to bring it within closer reach; and
- Shelving and other accessories that slide out from cabinets.

Case study 2.3 – cabinet design

Simply following the accessibility code for cabinetry design will not lead to good results. For example, lowering wall cabinets above a counter reduces the amount of good storage space on the counter.

A blender or microwave may no longer fit anywhere in the kitchen. Even an individual who uses a wheelchair wants to have small appliances conveniently located. When cabinets are lowered, the kitchen has to be rethought to accommodate small appliances, and, when cabinets are removed, additional storage needs to be provided to compensate. A full-height pantry cabinet, for example, may be a better way to provide accessible cabinet storage, leaving walls free for open shelving and racks for utensils, and so forth. Architect John Salmen had kitchen designer Jane Langmuir create custom cabinets for his own house that are deeper than usual to allow low storage at the back. The counters are supported by legs and base cabinets and can be removed if necessary. This approach provides very convenient storage for items used during food preparation and an attractive solution if knee space is required for seated work in the future. But custom work like this cannot be executed well without a lot of detailed drawings.

Flooring

Falling is one of the most common reasons for injury in building interiors, and floor coverings play a critical role in preventing slipping and tripping. Carpet is one of the most specified materials in commercial and institutional spaces. While it is comfortable under foot, it also reduces reverberation times, helping to reduce background noise and improve situational awareness. The wide variety of patterns and colors available for carpet also contribute to its effectiveness as a wayfinding cue. To ensure carpet selections support safety and usability for diverse users, including those with mobility difficulties, it is important to consider the following factors:

- Colors and patterns: use caution when selecting colors and patterns, especially in settings with users who may have low vision. Busy patterns and color combinations may lead to perception difficulties and cause a feeling of instability among users.
- Height of carpet pile/tuft density: low pile height and high tuft density make the carpet more firm and more usable by people using wheeled mobility devices, walking aids, and even those who shuffle their feet. Recommended pile height is between 1/4–1/2 in (6.4–12.7 mm). A beveled

transition is to be provided between carpet edges and adjacent floor surfaces with a ratio no greater than 1:2.

- Hypoallergenic carpet: carpeting with low volatile-organic-compound (VOC) ratings that incorporates bacteria guard, mildew guard, and non-allergenic fibers is best for the health of occupants.
- Carpet installation: carpet is safer and more user friendly if installed with a firm, rather than soft, cushion, pad, or backing underneath, or with no pad.
- Area rugs: it is best to avoid the use of area rugs if possible. When used, they need to be securely fastened to the flooring below to decrease tripping hazards.

Wood is a renewable resource and is aesthetically pleasing, easy to maintain, and resilient when installed in spaces that do not frequently get wet. When selecting a finish for wood floors, it is important to ensure that the finish is not too slippery or too shiny. Shiny floors can be visually distracting and reflections can be problematic for users with vision loss.

Tile floor coverings are available in a wide range of sizes, styles, finishes, and materials, including ceramic and stone. Although tile floors are easy to clean and durable, they can be problematic if the surface is too smooth and does not provide enough traction, particularly in areas that get wet. To increase safety, select tile with non-skid surfaces, especially in areas that may get wet such as bathrooms, kitchens, and mudrooms. Joints between tiles must not exceed 3/4 in (19.0 mm) to avoid causing difficulties for wheeled mobility device users or users with walking aids.

Other resilient flooring is an inexpensive, durable, and easy to maintain floor covering that, while often used in commercial settings, lends itself to use in a variety of settings including homes and offices. Resilient flooring is generally made from natural materials and includes types such as cork, linoleum, and vinyl composite tiles (VCT). The material properties of this flooring type make it mold and bacteria resistant, as well as make it easier to stand on for long periods in comparison to concrete, stone, or tile. Additionally, the non-slip finish supports safety, particularly in wet areas. Similar to carpet, caution needs to be exercised when selecting color combinations and patterns.[8]

Well-designed floor transitions are critical because of their importance to mobility for people who have a shuffling gait, use wheelchairs, or have vision impairments. They are also important for preventing accidents for all users. Abrupt edges should be avoided, and any difference in height between one floor surface and another should be kept to a minimum. Inadequate design of transitions is one of the leading causes of citations due to building code violations related to accessibility. Oftentimes, higher-end buildings tend to have more problems related to transitions compared with lower-cost buildings. This can be attributed to the presence of more luxurious materials where budgets are more significant.

Case study 2.4 – thresholds

In a large luxury residential building, the on-site building manager supervised the interior design of hallways. Her goal was to ensure a luxurious appearance. As a result, she insisted that all the thresholds be made from slabs of marble with abrupt edges. When the building was completed, the thresholds were cited for not complying with accessibility codes; they were too tall and did not have beveled edges. Since the carpet in the hallways was already installed, the developer had to remove the carpet and install beveled edges on all the thresholds that did not comply. Luckily, after carpet was installed in the hallways, many of the thresholds were compliant in height on that side of the door.

Slippery walking surfaces at entries is a common problem, often not noticed until a building has been constructed because it is hard to imagine how a material in a specification or drawing will perform in adverse weather conditions. All too often, problems with floors will be identified during construction or soon after, but nothing is done to address the problem until someone gets hurt. In most climates, water will be tracked into a building whenever it rains or snows, therefore, designers need to consider weather factors when specifying materials. The design of entries must address water, deploying materials and strategies that are not prone to being slippery when wet. The lack of attention to floor surface transitions that can become slippery is part of the reason why slips and falls are a major source of lawsuits against building owners and architects. Ideally, designers would avoid using slippery floor surfaces, but they are often under pressure by their clients to use luxurious materials like polished stone. Construction drawings and specifications really cannot convey the nature of the materials, so slippery surfaces are often overlooked until samples arrive during submittals. At this point, measures can be taken to ameliorate the problem before someone gets hurt. For example, a vestibule can be redesigned to include transitional entry flooring that will help dry shoes as individuals enter, which also can reduce the need for adding mats in bad weather to soak up the excess water that is tracked into the space.

Use of glass flooring and stair treads is a growing trend that needs to be reconsidered, especially near entries. Although these materials are designed not to be slippery under dry conditions with special surfaces and coatings, they may still be slippery once water is tracked on them.

Case study 2.5 – glass stairs

A major international retailer uses glass floors at the entry on monumental stairs of their stores. In their New York City stores, they have

2.19 Carpet on glass floor and stairway in retail store

to cover all the glass with segments of carpet when it is raining or snowing to prevent customers from slipping (see Figure 2.19). Architects have to make prevention of accidents a priority over the creation of "impression" spaces at building entries.

Acoustic control

In inclusive design, it is essential that all the senses receive adequate attention to satisfy the Goal of Awareness. Yet the acoustic environment is one of the most neglected areas of design. Acoustics contribute significantly to the experience of the built environment by assisting with orientation, location identification, and situational awareness. When planning for acoustic controls, it is important to consider the following:

- The space's purpose;
- The number of occupants;
- The length of time occupants spend in the space;
- The activities that take place in the space; and
- The space's location within the building.

At one time or another, a significant percentage of the population will experience some form of hearing loss, either temporary or permanent. As a result, acoustic control is important in all types of spaces, including residences, offices, and schools. There are three acoustic design strategies important for the practice of inclusive design:

- Controlling background noise;
- Ensuring speech intelligibility; and
- Reducing interference from mechanical and electrical systems.

Reducing background noise creates the baseline for a good acoustic environment. Background noise not only distracts all users from their activities but also requires people to raise their voices when talking to others, affecting the quality of interpersonal communications. Further, some individuals with disabilities, like people on the autism spectrum, become agitated with excessive background noise. Those with high tone hearing loss, like most people over the age of 75, will find that they have a hard time understanding the speech of others when background noise is excessive, like in busy restaurants. Speech intelligibility can be enhanced by the acoustic environment. A space with low reverberation times will sound "dead" and speech will not be clear as sound degrades too quickly. A space with high reverberation times will produce too much noise to hear critical information. Sound interference can be created by equipment like loud air conditioning or buzzing lighting fixtures. Light fixtures, air handling systems, and even plumbing can produce unwanted noise. The performance of assistive listening systems can be compromised by electrical interference from equipment that cannot be predicted.[9]

While architects cannot always anticipate these challenges during the design stage, there are solutions to lessen their negative effects. Reduction of background noise from outside the building can be accomplished by providing good acoustic separation and careful window selection. Additionally, reverberation can be reduced by installing carpeting, and in residential environments, by lining draperies. The arrangement of seating and furniture can also affect acoustics within a space. *Sociopetal* seating arrangements, which provide direct visual contact among individuals, encourage social interaction and provide good sight lines for conversation (see Figure 2.20). In offices, barriers between workstations are optimally made of sound absorbing materials and at least 64 in (1625 mm) in height. Finally, ensuring heating and air conditioning systems are quiet also supports good acoustic control within a space.[10]

Both common sense and scientific research emphasize the importance of good communication in education and interpersonal relationships, but somehow, the building community in many societies has not put value on this aspect of design. Although acoustic consultants are available, they are usually hired only to assist and evaluate designs when acoustics are known to be a critical factor for the success of a project, for example, in a performing arts space or open office environment. Even then, their advice is not always heeded.

Buildings with high background noise levels due to lack of sound absorptive materials, proportions that cause high reverberation times, lots

2.20 Sociopetal seating arrangement in university residence hall

of sounds from people talking, or exposed noisy equipment will interfere with the perception of human speech. Such spaces could be planned so that acoustic control can be added after the fact if needed and contribute to the aesthetics rather than detract from them, or provided with flexible acoustic treatment like hanging acoustic panels (see Figure 2.21).

Another problem is exposed mechanical systems, particularly air handling ducts. Good specifications ensure that mechanical equipment and distribution ducts and registers will not generate too much noise, and a budget is needed to fine tune the systems if they do not perform as expected.

Sign systems

As introduced in the wayfinding section, adequate signage complements a clear building layout and circulation system. Proper signage assists users with orientating themselves within the space, finding their destinations, and identifying key locations along the way. Effective signage systems also account for flexibility and can be changed easily and inexpensively. When approaching

2.21 Suspended acoustic treatment in university presentation space

signage inclusively, the following are a few recommendations to ensure the system is usable by as many people as possible:

- Readable from expected viewing distance and not obstructed by objects so people with limited vision can get close to read them;
- High contrast of characters on background;
- Does not produce glare and is protected from reflected glare;
- Provides all information in visual and tactile and/or audible format, including room purpose wherever signs provide room numbers;
- Selected signage uses pictograms and/or more than one language;
- Directory lists building occupants and room numbers under an organizational heading;
- Signage at intersecting routes are perpendicular to the direction of travel from all approaches to the intersection;
- Signage at intersecting routes provides navigation information (e.g., arrows guiding to range of room numbers, organizational headings, areas of primary functions);

- Selected signage links to additional online resources (e.g., QR code);
- Smart signage is provided on the premises (e.g., signs with radio frequency identifiers, near field communication, or other technology that allows communication with a personal computing device);
- Signage located in dark areas or outdoors are backlit, reflective, and/or directly illuminated; and
- Interactive model or plan of the building is available that can provide information through speech, text, or tactile media.[11]

Case study 2.6 – interactive wayfinding

Touch Graphics, in partnership with the Center for Inclusive Design and Environmental Access (IDeA Center), has developed a technology for creating interactive touch-sensitive models and maps (see Figure 2.22). Through several cycles of prototype development and testing, the partners established that these devices improve navigation for people with vision impairments by helping them to learn complex

2.22 Talking map at the Perkins School for the Blind by Touch Graphics Inc. and the University at Buffalo IDeA Center

sites. A raised line plan is mounted as an overlay on a touch-sensitive display. Three-dimensional building models can also be fastened to the overlay. Through a proprietary technology, sensors transfer the location of touches to the display. Information about the place touched can then be presented to the user through speech, text display, or even refreshable Braille. Users can explore the models and maps on their own, or be prompted in a sequence of tasks to learn the building or campus. One installation included an interactive game designed to make users familiar with the facility. A new installation is planned that will allow users to drill down and retrieve many other kinds of information like scheduled events at specific locations, descriptions of activities like art exhibits, or historical information on the building.

Furniture and fixtures

Essential to the process of designing through an inclusive lens is specifying furniture and fixtures that support user comfort, safety, and usability. These considerations happen at two scales during the planning process: layout and selection. When planning a furniture layout, key considerations include the following:

- Using sociopetal seating organizations;
- Providing enough room to accommodate several different furniture arrangements where long-term occupancy will occur;
- Integrating space for wheelchair users into the seating arrangement; and
- Providing more than one path of travel through each room without disrupting the viability of conversation and room activities.[12]

During the furniture selection process, it is important to consider the following attributes:

- Ergonomic design;
- Demand low physical effort for use;
- Options for adjustability (e.g., surface/seat height, seat back slant, removable/retractable armrests);

■ Flexibility in use (e.g., reconfigurable, removable parts to allow for knee clearance);

■ Made of sustainable materials; and

■ Materials support human comfort (e.g., low-glare surfaces, breathable upholstery/seating fabrics).[13]

These considerations all support the notion that the user has to adapt as little as possible to the furniture and fixtures used; instead, the furniture and fixtures adapt to the meet the needs of diverse users with a wide range of needs.

What are the design considerations for primary and supporting spaces?

Individual spaces are discussed in a scalar manner, beginning with assembly and performance spaces and culminating in restroom facilities.

Assembly and performance spaces

Depending on the size of the venue, wayfinding is an important consideration. Similar principles apply to these spaces as to the building as a whole. A key difference is the density of occupancy. Adequate room for circulation becomes increasingly important as the size of the space decreases, especially in spaces that serve larger numbers of people using wheeled mobility devices or who may be carrying large personal belongings. Designing circulation in such a way that the intermittent movement of others minimizes distractions for seated listeners/viewers is also a consideration.

Lighting, acoustics, and environmental control systems cannot be overemphasized in the context of designing inclusive assembly and performance spaces. Keep in mind that auditory and visual acuity are not binary, that is, deaf vs. hearing, or blind vs. sighted; vision and hearing exist on a continuum of abilities. As such, the qualities of visual and auditory environments can have tremendous impacts on occupants with small and modest visual or hearing impairments. Of course, all general principles of lighting and acoustics come into play, including the size, proportions, and form of the room, the finish materials, and the technologies used. Though it is often a goal, inevitably, light and sound will not be perfectly uniform throughout the space. This can be used purposefully, if communicated to attendees through a customer service system prior to reserving seats or immediately upon arrival, so that people can select which zones may provide them with the best experience. For this to occur, however, the architectural design team needs to work closely with the lighting and acoustic consultants and the facility management team in order to provide guidance on seating options.

The design of the thermal environment can also affect a wide range of audience members and performers. The practice in many venues is to "supercool" the space in anticipation of the arrival of occupants. While many returning audience members may know to wear layers of clothing, first-time guests with certain health conditions can experience discomfort or threats to well-being as cool temperatures rise rapidly to warmer temperatures as the space reaches occupant capacity. The selection and design of the HVAC systems is one factor. In some applications, for example, radiant floor systems provide more even temperatures than forced air systems. Other strategies may include creating microclimates that are more stable or more easily controlled for temperature-sensitive occupants, selecting flooring and seating materials that assist in maintaining stable body temperatures, or providing customer service options, such as warm clothing or personal heating/cooling devices, to patrons.

Classrooms and offices

The design opportunities and challenges seen in assembly and performance spaces, like lighting and acoustics, remain relevant for classrooms and offices. One difference between these spaces and large assembly spaces is size and complexity. The more important difference, however, is the degree of user control – actual and perceived – over classrooms and offices. Primary occupants often think of these spaces as their own territory, for example, "my office," and frequently exert authority over who enters, what furnishings and objects reside in the room, how they are organized, and the temperature, lighting, and sounds in the room. The territorial behavior that is inevitable in such spaces elevates the importance of both involving end users throughout the design of these spaces and designing for flexibility. Over the life span of the building, classrooms and offices will invariably host multiple "owners." Therefore, the specification of finishes and furnishings must accommodate a range of needs and preferences over time. Commensurately, specifying a variety of task, workstation, and seating types has become common practice for many elementary schools, college classrooms, and office spaces, as it affords diverse ways of working, for example, individually or in teams, standing or sitting, and diverse users, for example tall or short, relaxed or active, near-sighted or farsighted.

As previously stated, occupants also need to possess some degree of control over temperature, daylighting, and electric lighting, though the degree of control intertwines with other budgetary and design factors. The ultimate aims are to enhance work efficacy, improve environmental performance and energy efficiency, and foster self-determinism.

Though seemingly simple, classrooms require a close understanding of diverse learning needs and preferences. Some people are "visual learners," others are "auditory learners," and still others are "tactile learners," each preferring to take in, process, and present information through a particular modality. This becomes more critical among students with hearing or visual impairments, students with physical disabilities, and students with cognitive and emotional challenges, including both child and adult learners. Students with attention deficit or hyperactivity disorders, as well as students with dyslexia or other learning disabilities, also possess distinct educational needs and challenges. Instructional format and classroom design can play a sizable role in fostering or hindering learning. Acoustics, lighting, and furniture matter greatly. So, too, does the spatial and material flow into, out of, and through a classroom. Many students on the autism spectrum, for example, benefit from the thoughtful design of transitional and threshold spaces, as the relationship between the corridor and the classroom in conventional school designs can feel jarring; the same is true when designing classroom activities and activity centers. The key point for the architect is to understand the range of learners a classroom might contain and design both universal elements, such as noise control, and adaptable features, such as movable furniture.

Retail and commercial spaces

Whether in a grocery store, a hairstyling studio, a clothing shop, or a restaurant, self-determinism is a core element of a positive shopping experience. This includes the ability to find information and compare options, find and test those options, and, if desired, easily make a purchase. Retailers and service providers can fail in one or more of these areas; so, too, can designers of commercial and retail spaces. Understanding how people seek, interpret, and use information is key. From an inclusive design standpoint, it is recommended that information be supplied in multiple locations and media – for example, online, on-site, in print, in audio. Information also needs to include what products and services are available to target audiences, such as right- vs. left-handed users, people with sensory impairments, and families with small children. While much of this points to the design of customer services or to the design of products that retailers choose to carry (neither of which is under the purview of the architect), the design team needs to ask questions of the client regarding its corporate and customer service culture, which has implications on how the space is designed. Are customers primarily responsible for making decisions, or are they aided by staff? To what extent does the shopper handle or interact with the merchandise? To what degree are consumers in charge of the payment process? Answers to each of these questions have implications on the layout of spaces, product placement, and the building technologies specified.

Dwelling spaces

Few spaces are more diverse in context, typology, construction materials, finishes, furnishings, and makeup of occupants than dwellings. The variety increases if we expand the view to include not only private homes, duplexes, and apartments but also transitional housing, hotels, long-term health facilities, and other habitats.

Inhabitants use and interact with dwelling spaces more intimately than any other space type. Dwellings are places of child raising and elder care; places of solitude, partner intimacy, and gatherings of friends and family; and places for cooking, sleeping, and bathing. Homes are an extension of the values, behaviors, tastes, and personalities of its occupants. As the varied and complex phrase "being at home" implies, a home is part of the identity and psyche of its residents. A home with design elements that support physical, emotional, and cognitive aspects of its inhabitants can foster self-actualization, self-worth, and self-efficacy, while a home whose design impedes physical, emotional, and cognitive well-being can diminish not only one's value in self but also an individual's or family's role in society.

From an inclusive design perspective, task areas in residences, such as kitchens and bathrooms, need added attention. Activity spaces need to be designed in ways that promote flexible or adaptable use for children and older adults, people with low or no vision or hearing, men and women, very tall people and those who are shorter in stature, and right- and left-handed users. Adequate and adjustable lighting is key, as is variability (or adaptability) in the height and size of work surfaces and the height and operability of appliances and fixtures (see Figure 2.23).

Designers need to reflect on all potential occupants, not just the current or intended occupants, including visitors and future residents. Consider how space and personal belongings are stored, exhibited, and used by a wide variety of potential users, including those with different cultural backgrounds. A home is not simply a shelter; a home is a place of personal memories and artifacts that evoke those memories. A home is a place where people both protect and display a range of artifacts – from furniture to clothes, family photographs to collectibles, books to advanced technologies – a place where people both protect and display themselves. Design techniques for balancing privacy and presentation of identity include the following:

- Mapping the activities of individual occupants throughout the day;
- Mapping the social and spatial relationships among occupants;
- Listing the various ways that domestic tasks, such as preparing food, can be done; and
- Listing the factors that influence the performance of domestic tasks, such as height, strength, dexterity, eyesight, hearing, and cognition.

Inclusive housing must also address social change. Homes last a long time and, at some time, are likely to house one or more persons with disabilities. With increased life expectancy and population growth, designing for the last half of the life span – the second 50 years – is becoming more and more important since no society can afford to re-house all its older citizens in new buildings. Most older people want to remain living in their home as long as possible. To design for aging in place, a home has to be planned for the eventuality that a resident will no longer be able to use stairs. The Lifetime Homes program that the Rowntree Foundation in the United Kingdom developed was the first program to promote the idea of "visitability" – home design that can accommodate visitors with disabilities and that can be easily adapted for a resident with a disability. The basic elements of homes designed for the life span include the following:

- A minimum of one no-step path to a no-step entry that can be at the front, side, rear, or through a garage (1/4–1/2 in [6.4–12.7 mm] threshold);

2.23 Kitchen in the LIFEhouse, a universally designed home developed by New American Homes in Antioch, Illinois

- No-step access to patios, balconies, and terraces (1/4–1/2 in [6.4–12.7 mm] threshold);
- Doorways that have at least a 34 in (865 mm) wide clear opening with appropriate approach clearances;
- Door handles that are 34–38 in (865–965 mm) from the floor;
- Hallways and passageways that are 42 in (1,070 mm) clear minimum;
- Access to at least one full bath on the main floor with reinforced walls at toilets and tubs for the future installation of grab bars;
- Kitchen cabinetry that allows a person to work in a seated position;
- Light switches and electrical outlets 24–48 in (610–1,220 mm) from finished floor;
- Stairways have tread widths at least 11 in (280 mm) deep and risers no greater than 7 in (180 mm) high;
- Good lighting throughout the house including task lighting in critical locations (e.g., under kitchen cabinets);
- Non-glare surfaces;
- Contrasting colors to promote good perception of edges and boundaries;
- Clear floor space of at least 30 in (762 mm) × 48 in (1,220 mm) in front of all appliances, fixtures, and cabinetry;
- Front-loading laundry equipment;
- Ample kitchen and closet storage or adjustable shelving within 28–48 in (715–1,220 mm); and
- Comfortable reach zones.[14]

The Canadian Mortgage and Housing Council developed the concept of "Flexhousing" to accommodate differences in family needs over a life span and differences in neighborhood demographics. Flexhousing plans can be easily converted from a single dwelling to two dwellings and back again.

Restrooms and bathrooms

Ensuring health and safety are primary concerns in designing restrooms and bathrooms. This includes ways to diminish the likelihood of slipping, particularly when floors and surfaces are wet from use or cleaning, as well as providing adequate supports and options for transferring to/from toilets, showers, and other fixtures. Reducing the growth and spread of bacteria and viruses can help promote public health. This can be achieved through the design of easily maintained and fast-drying surfaces, the utilization of antimicrobial materials such as copper, and the specification of fixtures, for example, faucets, paper dispensers, and door hardware that both minimize human contact and reduce the harboring of germs.

Privacy and security are equally important. Women, young children, and people with physical, sensory, and cognitive impairments can be especially vulnerable to verbal harassment or physical assault if the interior and immediate surroundings of restroom and bathing facilities are not thoughtfully designed. Lighting, lines of sight, acoustics, and security hardware need to be considered and designed from the vantage point of vulnerability. Occupants need to both *be* safe and *feel* safe.

Cultural norms and taboos, in part, govern perceptions of privacy and safety. In many architectural projects, it is sufficient to understand the dominant cultural context. For other projects, designing a terminal in an international airport, for example, which likely serves hundreds of different ethnicities, knowing the variety of cultural groups that might use the space, each with its own practices of toileting and ablution, is important. Cultural change is also to be considered. Growing immigrant populations, aging communities, and changing attitudes toward gender all come into play.

There is an array of codes in all countries that apply to the design of public restrooms and private bathrooms. Accessibility codes emphasize the design of spaces and features for people using wheeled mobility devices, such as wheelchairs. Of course, these codes need to be met, but a more inclusive view of restroom design evokes questions about age, gender, and culture, often embedded in plumbing codes or public health ordinances. Recent debates, particularly in the United States, have pointed to the shortcomings of designing for gender as a binary construct (male vs. female), and the challenges and stigmas that transgender individuals face in this context. Caregivers, such as parents of young children or adult children of elderly parents, face a similar difficulty in assisting their loved ones in restrooms when the two people are of opposite genders. Cultural differences also play a role in preferences for types of bathroom fixtures and equipment, for example, squat toilets versus seated toilets or use of paper for cleaning versus use of water. Few areas of design call for more innovation and humane design than restroom facilities.

Notes

1 Gago, E. J., Tariq Muneer, M. Knez, and H. Köster. "Natural Light Controls and Guides in Buildings: Energy Saving for Electrical Lighting, Reduction of Cooling Load." *Renewable and Sustainable Energy Reviews* 41 (2015): 1–13.

2 Gago, E. J., Tariq Muneer, M. Knez, and H. Köster. "Natural Light Controls and Guides in Buildings: Energy Saving for Electrical Lighting, Reduction of Cooling Load." *Renewable and Sustainable Energy Reviews* 41 (2015): 1–13; and Lechner, Norbert. "Heating Systems." In *Heating, Cooling, Lighting: Sustainable Design Methods for Architects.* Somerset: Wiley, 2014.

3 Bellia, Laura, Fabio Bisegna, and Gennaro Spada. "Lighting in Indoor Environments: Visual and Non-Visual Effects of Light Sources With Different Spectral Power Distributions." *Building and Environment* 46.10 (2011): 1984–1992.

4 Lechner, Norbert. "Heating Systems." In *Heating, Cooling, Lighting: Sustainable Design Methods for Architects.* Somerset: Wiley, 2014; and ASHRAE. "Ashrae Standard 55–2013." In *Thermal Environmental Conditions for Human Occupancy*, 2013.

5 Lechner, Norbert. "Heating Systems." In *Heating, Cooling, Lighting: Sustainable Design Methods for Architects.* Somerset: Wiley, 2014; and Wargocki, Pawel, David P. Wyon, Jan Sundell, Geo Clausen, and P. Ole Fanger. "The Effects of Outdoor Air Supply Rate in an Office on Perceived Air Quality, Sick Building Syndrome (SBS) Symptoms and Productivity." *Indoor Air* 10.4 (2000): 222–236.

6 Steinfeld, Edward, and Jonathan R. White. *Inclusive Housing: A Pattern Book: Design for Diversity and Equality.* New York: W. W. Norton & Company, 2010.

7 Steinfeld, Edward, and Jonathan R. White. *Inclusive Housing: A Pattern Book: Design for Diversity and Equality.* New York: W. W. Norton & Company, 2010.

8 Steinfeld, Edward, and Jordana L. Maisel. *Universal Design: Creating Inclusive Environments.* Hoboken, NJ: John Wiley & Sons, Inc., 2012.

9 Ashburner, Jill, Laura Bennett, Sylvia Rodger, and Jenny Ziviani. "Understanding the Sensory Experiences of Young People with Autism Spectrum Disorder: A Preliminary Investigation." *Australian Occupational Therapy Journal* 60.3 (2013): 171–180.

10 Steinfeld, Edward, and Jordana L. Maisel. *Universal Design: Creating Inclusive Environments.* Hoboken, NJ: John Wiley & Sons, Inc., 2012.

11 Steinfeld, Edward, and Jordana L. Maisel. *Universal Design: Creating Inclusive Environments.* Hoboken, NJ: John Wiley & Sons, Inc., 2012.

12 Steinfeld, Edward, and Jordana L. Maisel. *Universal Design: Creating Inclusive Environments.* Hoboken, NJ: John Wiley & Sons, Inc., 2012.

13 Gossett, Andrea, Mansha Mirza, Ann Kathleen Barnds, and Daisy Feidt. "Beyond Access: A Case Study on the Intersection Between Accessibility, Sustainability, and Universal Design." *Disability & Rehabilitation: Assistive Technology* 4.6 (2009): 439–450.

14 Steinfeld, Edward, and Jonathan R. White. *Inclusive Housing: A Pattern Book: Design for Diversity and Equality.* New York: W.W. Norton & Company, 2010.

chapter 3

Construction

The pre-design and design phases promote, but cannot ensure, project success. The construction phase of a project *always* presents both challenges and opportunities. Buildings are complicated. Changes arise. This chapter, therefore, discusses key phases and features of construction that contribute to the well-being and experiences of building occupants.

How is inclusive construction different from conventional construction?

Most inclusive design features can be built with conventional methods and materials, but they still differ from conventional construction for two reasons: (1) inclusive design involves a quest for innovation, that is, building differently, and (2) it requires a high level of quality control in execution. Ensuring that final buildings incorporate inclusive design requires anticipating the problems that will arise, preparing in advance to minimize such problems, and developing a communications process to resolve them when the inevitable occurs. Thus, it is useful to contemplate the issues that may arise in construction, and identify strategies to use during the construction process to manage them.

The goals of inclusive design imply adopting innovative products and construction details that may be unfamiliar to the typical building contractor. Resisting innovative ideas is often due to fearing the unknown. In particular, resistance to inclusive design might stem from a concern that it conflicts with achieving other design goals. In building construction, such goals may include aesthetics, sustainability, economy, security, and climate resilience. Once construction gets underway, the unfamiliarity of inclusive design features can also lead to delays, problems of execution and, ultimately, change orders that compromise achieving inclusive design goals. For example, without sufficient lead-time, it may not be possible to find and incorporate products that meet both the goals of inclusive design and other design goals.

The first Universal Design Goal, "Body Fit," is a useful vehicle for illustrating these problems. Generally, a one-size-fits-all approach will not support reaching this goal. Conventional building design seeks to standardize products and features to reduce construction complexity and create a coordinated aesthetic statement, but inclusive design is about accommodating difference. This often leads to more diverse products and greater attention to specific needs. Ensuring that people of very different statures can use products effectively, for a wide variety of activities, requires thinking differently about even the most mundane products. If designers and contractors do not know how to create inclusively designed environments, they may be, understandably, unwilling to risk achieving a closer body fit because they fear it will cost more, look ugly, or result in delays during construction.

Case study 3.1 – water fountains

Conventional accessible construction might include water fountains at one "accessible" height. The conventional accessible water fountain is too high for small children and too low for tall adults, so they do not alone address the Goal of Body Fit. Dual-height water fountains often reconcile the needs of ambulant and non-ambulant users: one fountain or spigot for wheelchair users and one for ambulatory adults (see Figure 3.1). This is an inclusive design solution, but this idea can be taken one step further to address a broader population by providing three heights: one for small children and adults of extremely small stature; one for wheelchair users, larger children, and adults of small stature; and one for adults of large stature. This would be appropriate in facilities that have a high volume of visitors and serve a diverse population. Since three water fountains would be excessive in buildings where the demand for them is low, inclusive design might include a different type of water fountain, that is, one with flexible spout heights. Such fountains are not yet widely available, but an architect or designer could develop a customized solution. Further, when considering all the other Goals of Universal Design, the fountains may

3.1 Dual-height water fountains with bottle filler

also include additional features, like a water bottle filler for filtered water (Health and Wellness) and a low spigot for filling dishes for pets and service animals (Social Integration). Alternately, facilities may provide water in an entirely different way, for example, recyclable water bottles or a filtered water dispenser. Each building has different needs. For example, the triple-height approach might be appropriate in a major transit terminal that serves people of all ages. The adjustable approach may be more appropriate in a worksite with a diverse workforce. The water bottle dispenser may be the best strategy in a hotel, where guests can take filtered water back to their rooms or with them when they leave for the day.

An inclusively designed building will often have several new and different products and features, requiring designers, contractors, and other stakeholders to review the construction documents and manufacturer's installation details carefully. To communicate effectively to the contractor and trades, the designer needs to consider all the issues unfamiliar products and features might raise during construction, give care to address them thoroughly in the construction documents, and pay careful attention to the construction project itself.

Quality control critically ensures that poor construction does not compromise the usability of products and features. There are many reasons why the best intentions of designers can be undone during the construction phase of a project. These include taking too much leeway with field tolerances, uncovering unforeseen conditions in the field, and failing to give enough attention to the construction documents, particularly the details of design for disability.

Contractors and building regulatory officials who inspect the work may be knowledgeable about building code requirements, but often, they are not familiar with the rationale and background for those requirements. For example, research demonstrates that the maximum slope for ramps of 1:12 or 1:10 is too steep for many people with disabilities, and exceeding these maximums for any reason excludes an *even larger* proportion of individuals. Yet many design professionals and code officials often find, and approve, slopes exceeding requirements in the field because they believe that a slight variation would not make a difference (see Figure 3.2).

3.2 Renovated library with dual ramps. This library has dual ramps at the entry. One is designated as the accessible ramp because the other is slightly too steep.

Unforeseen conditions include finding hidden geological conditions or archaeological remains during excavation, addressing conflicts between drawings in real time to avoid halting construction, and substituting products to save money, time, or for aesthetic reasons. Sometimes these problems are unavoidable because they are simply unknown at the time of the design. When such conditions arise, however, it is important that the design and construction team consider inclusive design in the solution. The staff delegated to solve the problem need to be aware of the rationale for the original design, particularly the inclusive design features, in order to identify a solution that will not compromise them, if possible.

Strategy 3.1   Resolving unforeseen challenges

When previously unforeseen or hidden problems arise, consider how inclusive design thinking might assist, rather than simply focusing on the problem and solutions in isolation. Step back from the immediacy of the problem and place it in the larger context of project goals. What research and decisions of the pre-design and design phases might illuminate a viable and innovative solution?

Some contractors ignore construction documents and just construct building features as they have done in the past, or deviate from the documents simply because they think they have a better idea. To realize a good design, the development team has to ensure that inclusive design is just as important to the construction crew as it is to the design team and the client. The comparison to sustainable design is apt. Sustainable design requires attentiveness to every design detail that might affect the thermal performance of a building, and to construction practices that contribute to environmental degradation. Likewise, in inclusive design, contractors have to learn new ways of building even what appears to be the most ordinary of features, and to take special care adjusting to conditions that occur during the building process. Later in this chapter, we explore some of the most common challenges for inclusive design construction, but first, it is important to consider whom the construction team involves, what preparation and training they might need to avoid problems like those identified earlier, and what practices and strategies address these problems when they do occur.

Who should be responsible for universal design on the construction team?

There are many professionals involved in the construction process, and all contribute to inclusive design:

- Architect
- Owner's representative
- Construction manager
- Contractor and subcontractors
- Building trades
- Manufacturers' representatives.

Ideally, all these players are familiar with inclusive design. In reality, however, it is not likely that they will be unless they have had previous experience with such projects. They may even have some misconceptions about inclusive design based on problems they encountered in the past complying with accessibility codes. They simply may not understand why a product or feature will make a difference for the occupants. When not everyone is familiar with inclusive design, offering training, and clarifying roles and responsibilities during construction becomes important.

Architects administer the construction contract, an important role, during the construction phase of a project. This activity focuses on making sure that the construction in progress conforms to the construction documents. In small architectural firms, construction administration may often be the responsibility of the project designer. Having someone from the design team involved in construction administration is a good practice because they will be very familiar with the goals of the project and the rationale behind design decisions. In larger firms, a specialist may be responsible for construction administration, and this person may be unfamiliar with the details of the design. In this case, it is important for this individual to become very familiar with the specific project goals as they relate to inclusive design, because this person will be responsible for ensuring that the project goals are not subverted during construction. Additionally, the design team must establish a good communication process so that the individual responsible for on-site contract administration can confer with a knowledgeable person on the design team, if necessary. Prepare a list of inclusive design features in advance, so the individual inspecting the work can identify any necessary issues to bring to the design team's attention.

Small organizations and individual owners may participate in the construction process directly, but they will often rely on their architect to administer the construction contract. Larger organizations may have an in-house owner's representative, who may also be an architect. An owner's representative can play a very important role in inclusive design implementation. This is especially true if the architect's contract does not include construction administration, or services like information technology or security systems. The owner's representative will usually participate in the design process, even in hiring the architect and other design consultants. In that case, they will be very familiar with the goals of the project and may even be the champion of inclusive design within the owner's organization. Above all, the owner's representative can make sure that communications and decision making during construction do not slight inclusive design.

Owner's representatives sometimes assume responsibilities beyond the scope of the construction contract. For example, an owner may have an in-house interior design group. If that group is not familiar with the codes, or the inclusive design goals of a project, they can unwittingly subvert the design intent; for example, adding materials and design features that restrict circulation clearances for wheeled mobility users or altering acoustics. These team members may not discover such conflicts until construction is underway, or even finished. An owner's representative can coordinate the work of one design consultant with that of another, when not otherwise coordinated by the architect, to ensure they address such conflicts before they are problematic.

Not all projects have a construction manager (CM). Nevertheless, like the owner's representative, a CM can play a key role in inclusive design. CMs coordinate all the activities in a construction project. They schedule and plan the work, and play an important role in quality assurance. Thus, a CM can ensure that the contractor and building trades understand the project goals. They can also play an important role communicating between the contractor, the architect, and the owner. Scheduling is particularly important when a project uses innovative products that may take an unusually long time to order and ship. No one involved in a construction project likes delays. Thus, there will be pressure to substitute an inferior product, which is readily available, for an innovative product with good inclusive design features, especially if the latter are less expensive. A good CM will anticipate delays and make sure that the contractor and subcontractors place their orders for these products in a timely manner, so that they arrive on-site when needed.

Contractors and subcontractors are ultimately the professionals who bring the project to realization. It is important that they are aware of the inclusive design aspects of the project and understand the importance of following the construction documents. Good contractors will study the documents well in advance and discuss anything that they do not understand with the architect. They will also identify unusual products and features that may require a long lead-time to obtain, or necessitate special training for the construction crew. Good contractors will also pay close attention to the construction quality and bring problems to the attention of other team members in a timely way. Owner's representatives and construction managers can ensure that the contractor studies the documents carefully, and draw attention to any unusual products and features.

Building-trade workers, like carpenters, electricians, plumbers, and sheet metal workers, need to know when a higher standard of care is required to ensure that their work meets the project goals. If contractors and designers belittle, or de-emphasize, inclusive design goals, they are not likely to take sufficient care to ensure good work. If the design team clearly describes the purpose of inclusive design features to them, however, then they are more likely to do good quality work. They will also be more likely to bring field conditions that could compromise the design to the contractor's attention as soon as they discover them. Good subcontractors and trade workers, who are knowledgeable about construction details, can be strong partners in developing better inclusive design solutions, but they can do so only if they understand the goals and priorities of a design project, and are given the opportunity to contribute.

Strategy 3.2   Leveraging the knowledge of trade workers

Experienced trade workers possess deep knowledge and skills, far beyond the architect, and potentially beyond supervising subcontractors. If educated about basic principles of inclusive design and project goals, trade workers can serve as key allies in seeing emerging problems and developing on-goal solutions.

Manufacturer's representatives provide expertise on specific products like lighting and flooring. Companies are always introducing new products into the market. Manufacturer's representatives can make designers aware of those products that contribute to inclusive design goals. During the construction phase, they may be very helpful, as well, by providing advice on ordering the best product, identifying better alternatives to the products specified, providing advice on installation based on their experience, or training building-trade workers on proper installation of unusual products.

If a project utilizes expert consultants on safety, healthy design, and accessibility, it would be wise to include them, on an as-needed basis, in the construction phase of a project, should issues arise in the field. Experts can help resolve a problem in the best way possible because they are more likely to have encountered similar situations in the past.

What training does the construction team need?

If the construction team is unfamiliar with the practice of inclusive design, training on the topic will be necessary. We recommend that all the key members of the construction team receive training: architectural staff responsible for construction administration, construction management personnel, general contractor's key personnel, and the owner's representative. Training must include the following:

- A general orientation to inclusive design that provides a description of the inclusive design features in the building, with an explanation of their benefits;
- Attention to critical building code issues, including how inclusive design features of the building differ from minimum code compliance;
- A presentation on expected standards of quality and their importance, with examples; and
- A review of roles and protocols for communication.

This chapter serves as a good resource for a training program. The *innovative solutions for Universal Design* website (www.thisisud.com) is a tool designed to help select and keep track of these features during the design process. The construction phase training can also use this website.

A member of the construction team must be responsible for ensuring good communications among the project team. Although this is not technically related to inclusive design, it is important that the construction team knows what to do if they discover a problem, so it can be resolved without compromising the project goals. The architect, owner's representative, and/ or construction manager has to establish any necessary channels of communication to ensure that appropriate members of the design and owner's team review submittals and change orders.

What key details need attention?

The construction documents need to include and document any inclusive design features in order to minimize problems during construction. Then the team needs to monitor these features during the construction process in a timely fashion. In the design chapter, we provided an overview of inclusive design issues. The following section discusses a selected set of features, in detail, to illustrate the potential challenges that can arise during construction, and how to avoid them through careful design, good documentation, training, and timely monitoring. The following issues are not exhaustive, but they provide a good overview of anticipatory design and documentation.

Priority parking

Optimally, construction drawings provide dimensioned plans of priority parking spaces, especially accessible parking spaces, as well as the location of curb ramps serving those spaces, and illustrations of the signs and markings that regulations require. Use similar documentation for other types of priority parking. Sometimes, a site plan may designate only the number and location of such spaces. This practice leaves a lot to be decided during construction. Further, plans may include site amenities that are not even on the drawings, for example, facility signs, benches, and garbage receptacles. Since markings, signs, and amenities are typically not installed until the very end of a job, deadlines for completing construction often create even a greater potential that something will not be given enough thought or care in execution. Examples of this may include inaccurate line markings, or objects like utility posts or garbage receptacles, located in places that are barriers to wheeled mobility access and obstacles to people with vision impairments.

One of the most difficult problems during construction is ensuring that reserved parking spaces for people with disabilities, and access aisles serving them, are on nearly level ground, and that the curb ramps serving accessible parking are not too steep. It is often impossible to change the grading after the lot is completed. Thus, prior to the final site grading and installation of storm drainage, the construction manager and architect need to make sure that the parking lot grading plan is going to result in level ground at the reserved accessible parking areas.

Parking enforcement is a major problem wherever there are spaces reserved for a class of people. In the United States, each accessible parking space requires a sign at the head of the space, but not the adjacent access aisle (the no parking signs imply that no one can park in the entire area, not just the vehicle space). Some government officials and owner's facilities personnel think access aisles should have a "no parking" sign to prevent illegal parking in the aisles. This interpretation may not occur to the design team. If there are four accessible spaces, this may result in eight signs, with contradictory information. Pavement markings should be enough to control parking in the access aisles, but if the design team anticipates violations, there are other ways to prevent inappropriate use; for example, bollards. The parking facilities can also offer larger, "universal" spaces instead of separate access aisles. The larger spaces are preferable since they allow the driver to leave space for transfers on whatever side is most convenient, and, choose whether to back in or pull in forward. To avoid excessive and contradictory signage, it is important to ask for sign submittals, and to train construction managers to bring any proposals deviating from the drawings made by manufacturer's representatives to the proper development team members, before making substitutions, even if there is no cost implication.

Walking surfaces and ramps

One of the most common errors in accessibility regulation compliance, discovered after project completion, is excessive slope on walking surfaces and ramps. In inclusive design, meeting minimum codes is not sufficient since not all people can manage the maximum allowable slopes. In construction drawings, therefore, it is important to designate the maximum slope desired, and draw them accordingly, or, the contractor may default to the allowable minimum. It is impossible to build a concrete ramp or a walkway that has a uniform slope throughout. Thus, if drawings note specific slopes, for example,

1:12, it is likely that, somewhere along it, there will be a steeper portion. Use the following strategies to minimize such problems:

- ▓ Note "not to exceed" the target slopes on drawings to be clear about the desired end result;
- ▓ Designate a lower slope than the minimum, for example, 1:14 for a regulation that is 1:12, or, 1:20 for a regulation that is 1:16;
- ▓ Show the lower target slope in scale rather than relying on the dimension or note alone; and
- ▓ Inspect and measure slopes thoroughly with accurate measuring equipment.

Another common problem is abrupt changes in level along a walkway or at the bottom end of curb ramps. Some contractors make judgments in the field, when inspecting the work of their tradespeople, based on incorrect assumptions. One of the most common problems is that a lip at the end of a curb ramp will protect a curb ramp from water running up it onto the sidewalk. A good understanding of physics would dispel this assumption. Contractors also may believe that a small lip is not a barrier to wheeled mobility users, but even a small vertical displacement can make it difficult, or even impossible, for wheeled mobility users to mount a curb ramp. A vertical displacement can also be dangerous on a sidewalk that is otherwise smooth. Training for contractors can overcome these false assumptions. If they know what is expected, they are likely to be more rigorous in their inspections. Ideally, they will instruct their tradespeople about the importance of smooth transitions and surfaces.

Successful ramp and walkway construction relies on proper training. An important aspect of training is how to measure a sloping surface. There are many ways to measure slope, and accessibility regulations do not specify a standard approach. The tools and methods used will determine the results. For example, a short digital level will produce different results than a longer level since it is more sensitive to local deviations in a surface. A digital level, no shorter than 2 ft long (610 mm), or a laser-measuring device on a tripod, is recommended. It is also important to measure in several places because a sloped surface will not have perfectly consistent slopes everywhere, unless each segment is made of factory made components, like an aluminum ramp. Therefore, measure the running slope of a walking surface at fixed intervals, throughout its length, down its center. At some intervals, it is also desirable to measure the running slope at the two sides as well, since the slope may vary across the ramp.

Keep cross slopes to a minimum. The United States allows a maximum cross slope of about 2%. In concrete and masonry construction, deviations from this maximum are very common and hard to avoid. The previous dimensioning recommendations apply to this, but there is little range to maneuver since a slope of 1.5% is almost imperceptible compared with 2%. New digital, laser-measuring tools can be useful during construction to keep the variation as minimum as possible. For example, when pouring and smoothing concrete for a ramp, project a level laser beam across it to highlight any variations from level, and correct them before it is too late.

Fixing incorrect slopes on permanent ramps is very difficult and expensive, especially on concrete ramps. During ramp construction, therefore, it is advisable to monitor the construction very closely. Contractors and owners balk at ripping out concrete construction when the difference between the existing and target slope is very small. Keeping the target slope below code minima, as recommended earlier for walking surfaces and curb ramps, not only extends accessibility to a broader population, but also helps avoid difficult and expensive reconstruction. If a ramp or ramp section is slightly above the targeted inclusive design slope, but still under the code minimum, there is no problem with compliance.

Stairs

The most common problem in stair construction is uniformity of tread depth (running), riser height, and nosing projection. Codes generally allow variation of up to 3/8 in (9.5 mm) between the smallest dimension and largest dimension of all risers, or, all treads on the stairway. Since irregularity in tread and riser dimensions is a leading cause of stair accidents, striving toward "zero tolerance" is important. Stair construction often includes shortcuts. For example, a contractor may construct the stringers, or purchase prefabricated stringers, fasten them at the top, and simply cut down the bottom end to fit, leaving a shorter stair riser at the bottom. Another common error is fastening the stringer at the top without allowing for the thickness of the finished floor. This increases the height of the top riser. Most falls occur at the top and bottom, so avoid any irregularity at these locations. Check the uniformity in treads and risers by crouching at the top and sighting down the nosings. A large discrepancy will be apparent, but actual measurements may be necessary to determine small variations. Another common problem is the construction of railings. Drawings do not always include handrail details, such as the cross-sectional shape, leaving decisions on the handrail shape and dimensions to contractors. If construction documents do not provide details, an architect can provide and review a shop drawing before construction.[1]

Because of the precise dimensioning and careful detailing required on stairways, any deviations in the field are serious problems. In these instances, the only solution for stair geometry is demolition and reconstruction. Problems with walking surfaces and handrails may require replacement. Other features, like lighting, color, or texture, may be easier to fix.

Decorative or feature stairs often require shop drawings. The architect, contractor, and any relevant subcontractors need to check them carefully against the original drawings and specifications for additional details that may not have been included in the construction documents. Changes in material, color, texture, and lighting often occur during construction for aesthetic reasons; the design team often makes these changes independently of safety and usability criteria. For example, an owner's representative might seek to upgrade the quality of a space by changing the surface material. It is critical, therefore, to include stairs in the list of items that a team member knowledgeable about inclusive design, and, specifically stair safety, needs to clear during review and change order approval. Since building codes do not cover all the important stair safety features, approval by building code officials, or checking for code compliance alone, is not sufficient.

No-step entries in housing

In the construction of single-family homes, providing a stepless entry seems to be a huge hurdle for many contractors, although, in new commercial construction, contractors accomplish it every day. Since architects have limited involvement in mass-produced home construction, there is no one on-site to review the work. Thus, contractors and subcontractors have more leeway in how they build. Drawings for mass-produced houses lack detail, often not even showing the house in conjunction with the lot, except for a site plan that notes setbacks and walkway locations. Without detailed drawings showing how the building fits into the site, contractors have no guidance in determining the depth of the foundation or grading of the land around the perimeter of the building. This may lead them to fall back on their familiar approaches.

An additional problem is tradition in the homebuilding industry. Even when an architect or owner insists on it, builders are often resistant to including grade level access. The main objections contractors have to stepless entries include requirements for a step up from garages, the belief that water will leak into exterior doors, the need to keep wood away from the ground, and lack of experience with innovative solutions.

Some building codes still require one step between the ground floor of homes and garage floors. The origin of this requirement is unclear. Two possible explanations are that it prevents water from entering the home, or that it prevents carbon monoxide, which is heavier than air, from entering the home. The solution to both problems is to slope the garage floor toward the automobile entry door. Some building departments, however, may insist on the step so homebuilders must comply, requiring a ramp or lift to make the entry from the garage accessible. To avoid a lift or a ramp, an alternative entry could serve as the stepless entrance.

In the construction of commercial buildings, many techniques already exist to provide on-grade entries that prevent water penetration. Several successful methods used in housing include the following:

- Grading around the building to drain water away from the entry;
- Providing a canopy or overhang above the entry to reduce exposure to water;
- Putting a trench drain in front of the threshold to intercept any water that might collect near the door; and
- Designing a threshold and door to prevent wind-driven rain from entering under the door.

It is true that wood cannot be too close to the ground or it rots, but all that is needed to protect wood is a 6 in (155 mm) gap. In termite infested areas, install copper wire, which termites will not cross, or conventional termite shielding around the foundation.

Use simple, but unconventional, construction methods for housing construction to reduce the height of the first floor and bring it closer to grade, so that landscape grading provides the no-step entry. The most obvious construction method is a slab-on-grade foundation. Where a basement or crawl space is desired, a "reverse brick ledge," or notched foundation, can lower floor joists (see Figure 3.3).

Details like these are important to include in construction documents. If architects engage in construction administration, they must ensure that builders understand and agree to incorporate the included details, because the builders may simply think that the details are the same as what they traditionally build, if no one brings the differences to their attention.[2]

Another common issue involves selecting accessible, weather resistant, and energy efficient exterior doors. Most high performance exterior residential doors come with their own thresholds (or saddles). To ensure that they do not allow too much air infiltration, and prevent wind-driven rain from entering the building, these thresholds are often quite high. In fact, to prevent wind-driven rain, the bottom track of sliding doors has to be much

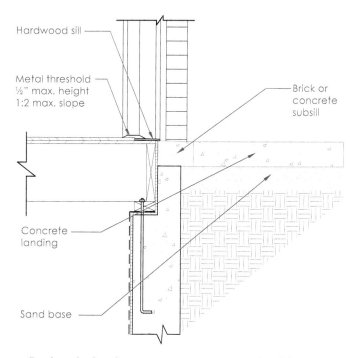

3.3 Foundation detail to achieve a zero-step entry using a reverse brick ledge

higher than many wheelchair users can roll over. Removal of factory-supplied thresholds will void the warranty of the doors; thus, contractors are reluctant to modify them. Accessibility requires special detailing (see Figure 3.4).

Strategies for ensuring accessible and weatherproof doors include the following:

- Carefully investigating the door products available;
- Developing a detail that accommodates a reduced threshold on both sides of the door;
- Recessing the track or saddle into the floor;
- Monitoring construction to ensure correctly installed doors, because even a height difference of 1/4 in (6.4 mm) above the maximum code can be inaccessible; and
- Providing positive drainage adjacent to the exterior side of the door.

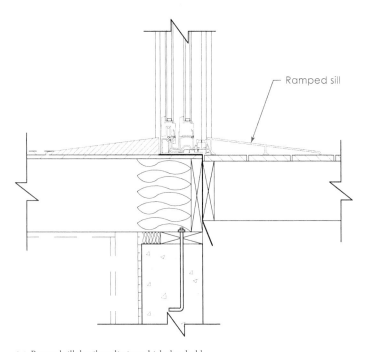

Ramped sill

3.4 Ramped sill detail to eliminate high threshold

Note that all these details are unusual and will require explanation to contractors.

Cabinetry

Adaptable cabinetry has not evolved very much since the 1970s. There are some good precedents, but the industry needs more affordable solutions. This is an area ripe for innovation. Adjustable heights for counters and cabinets would be a desirable feature for many households, if it were affordable. Because they are so rare, including adaptable cabinetry in a project requires special attention in construction documents. It is not that difficult to provide mounting brackets for wall cabinets at different heights, and modular based cabinets can be designed to allow homeowners, or janitors, to adjust the countertops to their preferred height. The international retailer IKEA produces a cabinet system that uses such installation practices, at reasonable prices.

Case study 3.2 – detailing cabinet assemblies

The practice of providing allowances in the construction contract for cabinets without details can lead to unanticipated problems during construction. In one project designed to serve people with severe disabilities, the architect specified that the wall cabinets have their lower shelf at 48 in (1220 mm). The contractor decided, with the approval of the architect, that since the upper shelves of standard cabinets would still be inaccessible to the tenants, they could make the wall cabinets shorter and save money. The result was that the top of the cabinets, which were unfinished, were visible to tall people, and made the kitchens very unattractive. If the contractor studied the completed installation drawings from an inclusive design perspective, this could have been avoided.

In many projects, contractors do not finish the floors under the base cabinets in adaptable kitchens. Removing base cabinets to provide knee clearance leaves the subfloor visible and requires new flooring installation. A similar problem arises when the backsplash for the countertop is a conventional size (ending at the underside of the counter). Lowering the countertop reveals an unfinished surface. An oversized backsplash, however, if fastened to the wall itself rather than the counter, will not leave an unfinished surface when lowering the counter. Avoiding these problems requires carefully detailing the cabinetry, and showing both installed conditions and adapted conditions. In other projects, the drawings simply state that the cabinets are adaptable, but all that it means is that the floor has been finished. Removing the cabinets and supporting the countertops requires skilled carpentry. Developing good details, and including them in the construction drawings, would eliminate this problem (see Figure 3.5). A cabinet manufacturer may be willing to discount the cost of custom cabinetry for a project if the company can benefit from an addition to its product line. Such collaboration may provide income to the designer.

Since adjustable height counters will hold sinks and vanities, it is important to plan for installing plumbing and electrical supplies that address height changes. Well-designed outlets, switches, drains, and water supply lines can easily accommodate such height adjustments, but it can become a major problem if it becomes necessary to change the height. Further, if removing underneath cabinets, the structural strength of the countertop has to be much greater to accommodate the span. Failing to address these details prior to construction will waste time working them out in the field. It can also result in change orders and increased costs.

Acoustic control

It is very difficult to imagine what the perception of sound will be like in a building that is not yet constructed. Drawings can easily assess a proposed visual environment, especially with contemporary CAD tools, at any designer's desktop, but comparable tools are not available in the architect's toolbox for assessment of the sonic environment. Perhaps this representation gap is the cause of the relative neglect for this important aspect of design. Thus, acoustic problems become evident only once a building is almost finished. At this point, what can be done about any problems in the building development cycle?

Pay far more attention to acoustics during the design stage. In addition, architects need to design spaces that can be modified easily to improve acoustic performance once problems are identified in construction, or shortly thereafter. In fact, they can plan spaces that can be customized for different kinds of uses and flexible for different types of events.

3.5 Adaptable bathroom vanity cabinet with removable base in Wounded Warrior home by Clark Realty Capital LLC

Case study 3.3 – the system and its elements

A school that serves people who are deaf and hard of hearing had a space for presentations designed. While the design team attempted to ensure the moving air in the duct runs would not generate too much noise, the mixing boxes turned out to be too small and produced too much unwanted sound for a facility like this. The example illustrates, that even with due diligence during the design phase, one element in the system can negatively affect the outcome of the whole.

When the design or construction team discovers such problems during construction, it is not too late to take action. Strategies for improving acoustics during or soon after construction include the following:

■ Adding sound insulation to reduce background noise generated outside a space or building;

■ Adding more sound absorbing materials to reduce reverberation, or sound reflecting materials to increase reverberation; and

■ Installing electronic measures like white noise generators or soundscape systems.

To ensure that there are resources available to address problems during construction, include a contingency in a building fit-out budget to address unanticipated noise problems.

Electrical and mechanical controls

As buildings incorporate more and more information technology, software-driven electrical and mechanical controls become increasingly critical for usability. Construction documents do not usually include the design of the user interface for these control systems, and designers do not regularly explain them to building owners or their representatives. Occupants face a bewildering array of controls, even in a simple classroom, or default settings they cannot overrun. If the design process fails to include selecting and evaluating the controls, then it may be impossible to correct these problems during construction without costly change orders. Most often, subcontractors make bids on projects based on assumptions about systems they would use, without considering the usability of the interfaces.

Case study 3.4 – thermal comfort scenario

A heating and air conditioning unit of a bedroom, in an assisted living facility, had a built-in delay to allow the heating coil to warm up before the fan started. The room occupants, many of whom had dementia, could not understand its operation. When it became cold, they would increase the temperature. When the fan did not start, they would increase it again, and so on. When residents left, the heat would come on and overheat the room. When residents returned, they would turn the temperature way down and the room temperature would then go to the other extreme.

Inclusive design can alleviate the problems with poor interface design. Some strategies to consider include the following:

- Conduct small usability studies, during either design or the construction process, when selecting specific products;
- Investigate software interfaces to ensure that controls allow building managers to make adjustments easily;
- In the construction specifications, specify and demonstrate control systems for lighting, heating and air conditioning, security, and other systems, either on-site or in showrooms, prior to final approval by the architect and owner; and
- Include training for occupants and adjustment of defaults during a commissioning phase of the project, immediately after construction.

Sign systems

One of the most common construction related problems with sign systems is non-compliance with accessibility code requirements for maximum mounting heights. Address this problem the same way as ramps, by specifying slightly lower heights, so that a minor variation of a fraction of an inch or a few millimeters will not make any difference. Such a dimensioning approach, however, may leave too much leeway for the contractor. They may put the signs too low. Thus, specify both a target height lower than the required maximum, and add a tolerance as well. For example, if the code maximum for mounting height is 60 in (153 mm) maximum, specify 58 in +/− 1/4 in. (147 mm +/− 5 mm).

What are the key issues in the construction process?

The previous examples are limited but, taken together, they identify key issues that need to be addressed during construction to control the quality of the work:

- Poorly executing details, usually caused by inadequate information in the construction drawings, mistaken interpretations of drawings and specifications, or poor quality assurance;
- Deviating from dimensions in the construction drawings, and violating building codes resulting from adjusting dimensions to field conditions, careless work, mistaken beliefs about acceptable tolerances, or inattention to the drawings;
- Substituting products that are different from the specifications, due to unavailability of products, ill-advised value engineering, or beliefs that alternatives are better quality; and
- Discovering problems too late into the construction process, caused by lack of communication between members of the construction team.

How to maintain quality control during construction?

Monitor compliance with specified dimensions diligently

It is not a good idea to wait until completing a project to check for compliance with dimensions in the construction documents. Ideally, each trade knows what needs to occur, and can monitor its own work while underway. The general contractor, construction manager, and architect need to check the work of subcontractors during each phase to prevent potential deviations on important dimensions, and to catch any code violations before it is too late to do anything about them. Compliance is easier if the construction drawings build in a tolerance for deviation and adopt a higher level of accessibility for inclusive design than codes require.

Establish dimensional tolerances

Establish acceptable tolerances at the beginning of a construction project so that the contractor and building trades know what is expected. These tolerances have to reflect the nature of the built element. For example, a tolerance of +/−1/4 in (6.4 mm) might be appropriate for a turning area for wheelchair users, but a threshold height needs +/−1/8 in (3.2 mm). It would be wise to include a written list of tolerances in the construction documents. The following is a set of tolerances for common issues that occur in practice, with a rationale for each. Note that these tolerances reflect the opinions of the authors, and regulatory authorities may not accept them.

- Sloped walking surfaces, for example, ramps, curb ramps, cross slopes, beveled edges: +/− 0.2%. Rationale: Accepted industry tolerance is +/−1/4 in (6.4 mm) in 10 ft (3048 mm). This equals about 0.2% as a measure of slope. This is a minor amount and should have no impact on accessibility.
- Dimensions of parking bays, access aisles, and loading zones with adjoining spaces: +/− 2 in (50 mm). Rationale: No accepted industry tolerance exists. However, since wheelchair users can cross the line in open space, some deviation is acceptable, unless walls or other permanent construction confines the spaces.
- Changes in level along a walking surface and thresholds, for example, exterior walkways, floors, thresholds: +/− 1/4 in (6.4 mm) for overall height and none for an abrupt edge. Rationale: The accepted industry tolerance for paving on walking surfaces is +/− 1/4 in (6.4 mm) over a 10 ft (3048 mm) length. Adding more than 1/4 in (6.4 mm) to the 1/4 in (6.4 mm) standard would result in a condition that could be a serious barrier to wheelchair users, and a tripping hazard for ambulant people. Small-scale repairs, and rebuilding small sections of the surfaces, can help adjust walking surfaces. Threshold products are available that meet accessibility standards.
- Dimensions for mounting fixtures or accessories from a manufactured object to a wall, for example, grab bar clearances, water closet location, and protruding objects: + 1/4 in (6.4 mm) for maximum dimensions, − 1/4 in (6.4 mm) for minimum dimensions. Rationale: Accepted industry tolerances for steel-framed gypsum walls and, the worst condition, brick walls, are satisfactory. They would have little impact, if any, on accessibility.

■ Height dimensions measured to the finished floor, for example, height of operable equipment, knee clearance, and protruding objects: + 1/4 in (6.4 mm) for maximum dimensions, – 1/4 in (6.4 mm) for minimum dimensions. Rationale: Accepted industry tolerances for concrete floors, site built cabinetry are satisfactory. This would have little impact, if any, on accessibility.

■ Clear width, opening dimensions, and related clearances, for example, clear door width, "pinch points," width of knee space, and door maneuvering clearance: – 1/4 in (6.4 mm) (positive deviation improves access). Rationale: Accepted industry tolerance is 3/16 in (4.8 mm) for economy grade wood door frames; these dimensions also apply at "pinch points," where the opening can be less than 36 in (915 mm) for distances of up to 24 in (610 mm), and knee space clearances where 1/4 in (6.4 mm) clearances may apply (cabinetry). The 1/4 in (6.4 mm) dimension is more feasible for field measurements, as well. Note that current research demonstrates that wheeled mobility devices have increased in width since 1980. Door clearances should be wider than the current 32 in (815 mm) minimum, so only the smallest possible tolerance should be allowed.

■ Handrail or grab bar diameter: + 1/2 in. (12.7 mm), with no negative tolerance. Rationale: the International Codes Council and the Americans with Disabilities Act (ADA) 2010 Standards allow up to 2 in (50 mm) outside diameter, 1/2 in (12.7 mm) greater than the ADA Accessibility Guidelines (ADAAG) requirement of 1 1/2 in (38 mm) maximum. Other codes limit the minimum diameter.

■ Operating force, for example, doors, plumbing controls, and miscellaneous hardware: + 0.5 lb (0.2 kg) (negative deviation improves access). Rationale: Research on door opening force indicates that many people with disabilities have a great deal of difficulty overcoming the opening force of doors; only a very small additional tolerance should be allowed. Closers that are adjustable within code ranges are available so, at worst, meeting this requirement would usually mean only switching out a closer. There are conditions where prevailing winds require larger forces than allowed. Use windscreens and automatic openers in these locations.[3]

Leave nothing to interpretation

Construction drawings can provide all the details necessary to execute innovative features and avoid "default thinking" that is based on previous experience. Commensurately, contractors can be encouraged to consult with the architects whenever they do not have enough guidance. This also means that the architect needs to have staff who are accessible to address questions in real time, and avoid delays.

Plan coordination between trades and subcontractors
The actions of one building trade can affect the ability of another to complete their job properly. For example, a plumber has to install the rough-ins for sinks and lavatories in the right place for a carpenter to provide adaptable cabinetry. Electrical supply is needed in convenient locations for installing automated door openers. During construction, regular job site meetings can be effective in anticipating and preparing for upcoming work.

Develop a clear chain of communication
Product substitutions and alternative approaches from the construction drawings do not need to be discouraged, particularly if they lead to improved quality. Since the entire construction team will not be party to the rationale for innovative products and features, however, the contractor, subcontractors, and trades have to bring all proposed alternatives to the attention of someone who does understand the rationale. That might be the architect or the owner's representative.

Plan for making adjustments
Reserve part of the project budget and schedule for "breaking in" the building. Referred to as "commissioning" in the sustainable design world, it is a good concept to keep in mind for any construction project. This is a time to make sure all systems are working, and to make adjustments as needed. As more and more design projects include automated software controls systems, this period of the construction phase becomes more critical. At the same time, software provides an opportunity for more flexible interfaces for electrical and mechanical systems, and more people-centered approaches. This is discussed further in Chapter 4.

Anticipate problems and develop countermeasures
The most effective way to avoid problems with implementing inclusive design during construction is to anticipate them ahead of time, and develop a strategy to avoid them. Some issues can be addressed in the design phase,

including good research, product selection, detailed drawings, and good specifications. Some can be addressed in planning the construction phase, including organizing submittals through a clear and streamlined process, reviewing and approving submittals and change orders, meeting with the construction team regularly, and communicating with all members in a timely and responsive way.

Notes

1 International Code Council. International Building Code, Section BC 1009 Stairways and Handrails. International Code Council, Inc. 2015.
2 Steinfeld, Edward, and Jonathan R. White. *Inclusive Housing: A Pattern Book: Design for Diversity and Equality.* New York: W. W. Norton & Company, 2010.
3 Ballast, David Kent. *Handbook of Construction Tolerances.* Hoboken, NJ: John Wiley & Sons, Inc., 2007; and Steinfeld, Edward, Jordana Maisel, David Feathers, and Clive D'Souza. "Anthropometry and Standards for Wheeled Mobility: An International Comparison." *Assistive Technology* 22.2 (2010): 51–67.

chapter 4

Occupancy

Occupancy refers to the point in construction when a building is finally used for its intended purpose. During this time, building users – including individuals, employees, residents, and tenants – inhabit a facility and interact with the built environment by living in, working in, playing in, passing through, and/or visiting the space. Occupancy, however, does not mark the end of the design process. In fact, it triggers perhaps the most important phase of improving and maintaining an inclusive facility, further ensuring that occupancy results in meeting users' diverse needs. Occupancy assessments also add to architects', contractors', owners', and managers' understanding of how to improve other buildings and properties, including future projects. More specifically, accessibility assessments and post-occupancy evaluations systematically examine a building's construction and performance in order to evaluate compliance with codes, identify areas of success, and outline opportunities for improvement. Facility management practices regarding safety, maintenance, and operations help reinforce and support successful designs throughout the life span of a building. This section describes how to employ methods and procedures to create the most usable, efficient, and pleasant environments for occupants.

What is the "shakedown" period?

The shakedown period occurs immediately after a building is constructed, when minor glitches in policies, designs, and/or systems are identified and resolved prior to the site and facility becoming operational and occupied. The length of the shakedown period varies depending on the site's complexity and the diversity of users in the space. During this specified time, the design team and building owners may encounter unclear signage, inconvenient storage placement, or technological bugs. The goal is to identify as many of these fixes as possible, and as early as possible, in order to increase the likelihood of success once people occupy the building.

Accessibility assessments

The primary role of architects and designers is to create environments that are safe, usable, and meet the goals of their target users. Some design decisions, however, can unknowingly create barriers for subsets of the population by failing to address some of their needs. Such groups include people with physical or cognitive disabilities, caregivers, people of low socioeconomic status, children, and older adults. Unintentional barriers can be anything from a door that is too heavy to open, to stairs and passageways that block access for individuals who use a mobility device, to a poor layout and numbering system that causes people to get lost. Conducting an assessment during the shakedown period ensures that a site and/or building comply with applicable accessibility standards and regulations, and that a building and/or site will not unintentionally exclude people with disabilities. Features found not to be in accordance with regulatory requirements provide the groundwork for an action plan to mediate, modify, or remove barriers.

An accessibility assessment can occur at various stages throughout the design and construction process. Ideally, an initial review of drawings regarding accessibility criteria occurs during the design phase, when there is ample time to make revisions. Once construction is complete and the facility becomes occupied, an accessibility assessment can help ensure that suppliers, facilities managers, and users themselves place furniture and equipment in accordance with both applicable codes and factors of usability and convenience. For example, an assessment might reveal when furniture placement obstructs paths of movement or access to environmental controls (see Figure 4.1). Once a building is occupied, accessibility audits might also be needed if a lawsuit claiming an inaccessible building is filed. In these instances, opposing sides hire code experts, for example, architects or code officers, to conduct systematic assessments that document any features that are not in compliance with regulatory requirements. After reviewing and comparing these assessments, lawyers work to resolve the case through arbitration, settlement, or trial. Finally, for buildings that have been occupied for some time, an accessibility assessment can highlight areas that need improvement, thereby guiding renovation, maintenance, and management plans.

A noteworthy point is that accessibility requirements and assessments aim to eliminate fundamental barriers for people with disabilities, but they do not address usability and convenience issues for the broader population. Further, while these standards provide minimum requirements to accommodate people with disabilities, they do not inform designers how to provide optimum conditions for this group, nor do they address significant gaps in user capabilities, e.g., addressing sensory and cognitive disabilities. Building codes and standards focus primarily on access and egress, safety, and some health issues, like sanitation. They do not address the full range of issues related to usability, social integration, comfort, and wellness. Inclusive design is more comprehensive; therefore, the assessments that occur at the occupancy phase must be broader. In practice, inclusive occupancy and post-occupancy evaluations expand the reach of accessibility to a much broader population, as well as a wider range of objectives. Making environments more usable for everyone reduces the stigma associated with disability, while allowing a much broader segment of the population to use and enjoy facilities.

Commissioning building systems

When a new building is constructed, systems need to be checked to see if they are working properly before the owner takes possession, a phase called "commissioning." Commissioning is an important activity for realizing inclusive design, particularly as new and innovative technologies are being introduced into buildings. From a building occupant's perspective, the systems to check include the following:

- Lighting, including both electric and daylighting controls
- Acoustics
- Thermal comfort systems
- Electrical systems
- Plumbing fixture
- Public address systems, including assistive listening devices
- Built in computer systems
- Doors and windows
- Appliances and office equipment
- Emergency systems
- Security systems.

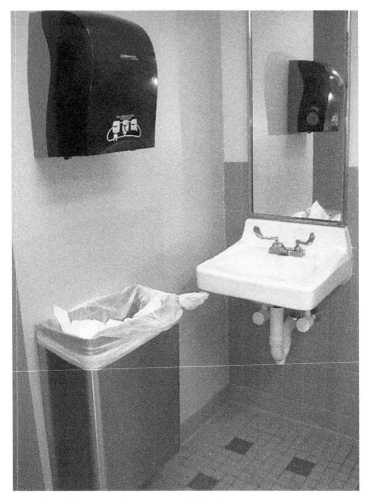

4.1 Trash can placement resulting in unintended obstacles to movement

It is not sufficient for design professionals to test the systems, as they are too familiar with how things work. Instead, the design team needs to recruit a diverse sample of building users to tour the building and operate all systems. Ideally, they will stay in the building and conduct routine activities for at least a day. Facilities managers can also schedule emergency drills. The focus needs to be on the usability and safety of "user interfaces" as well as the performance of all systems. This activity can be useful to identify equipment that is not working properly, unexpected problems, and unanticipated training needs.

It is important to note that every device or system that requires some adjustment by a user or maintenance employee has a "user interface." This term primarily applies to information technology, but even plumbing fixtures, windows, and doors have user interfaces. Can users operate door and window locks easily? Do they know how to turn on and shut down computer systems? New technologies are increasing the complexity of all building products and many potential problems are still unknown. For example, biometrics like retinal scanners and voice recognition are being used in security systems. Are they usable by people with unusual eye conditions or people with implants, or people with voice or hearing impairments? It can be embarrassing for an individual to have functional problems in public, not to mention the possibility of compromising the goal of enhanced security. During commissioning, building owners, managers, and designers can identify and remediate such problems before they may have an impact on productivity, independence, and user satisfaction.

Case study 4.1 – retrofitting lighting fixtures

In one building, light fixtures were controlled by presence sensors, but the time-out period was too short for sedentary workers. The lights shut down automatically when the workers did not move enough to keep them on. An adjustment to the time setting in these areas solved the problem. In the same building, new LED light fixtures, though commonly cool to the touch, produced enough heat to cause a vibration, which resulted in a buzzing noise as a loose piece of thin metal brushed against another. The longer the fixtures were on, the worse the noise became. Hundreds of fixtures had to be adjusted. It would have been better to do it before the owner took possession, and the cost would have been borne by the contractor or manufacturer, not the owner.

What is post-occupancy evaluation (POE), and what is its utility?

One way to measure the effectiveness of any environment is to observe the degree to which it enables and increases user performance. A post-occupancy evaluation (POE) is the process of systematically evaluating the performance of buildings after they have been constructed and occupied for a period of time. A POE is an established and validated research method in design for determining the effectiveness of building features. Therefore, POEs are not simply about documenting the features in a building, but about understanding how those features impact performance, for example, satisfaction and productivity. Most POEs involve a systematic investigation of user perceptions and viewpoints about built environments. This often includes surveys, focus groups, and/or interviews with various users of the building in order to learn about the features that work well, that present barriers, and that can be incrementally improved.[1]

There are three types of POEs. First, "indicative POEs" reveal the major strengths and weaknesses of a particular building's performance. These typically consist of selected interviews with knowledgeable informants, as well as a subsequent walk-through of the facility. Second, "investigative POEs" go into more depth, whereby objective evaluation criteria are compiled through performance standards and published literature on a given building type. Third, "diagnostic POEs" correlate physical environmental measures with subjective occupant response measures.[2]

Participants

The evaluator largely determines POE participants by the building's key stakeholders. Optimally, the target sample includes frequent users, including management, as well as visitors, if applicable. Studying both types of users allows a variation in exposure times, with frequent users more familiar with the building and, therefore, more likely to notice design enhancements. Engaging new users provides an assessment of the environment from individuals who are unbiased by long-term exposure and adaptation.

Performance measures

POEs differ from other evaluations of building performance in that they focus on the requirements of building occupants. Performance measures help evaluate whether an established goal was achieved. When evaluating the needs of building occupants, performance measures include those related to productivity, health, safety, security, functionality and efficiency, comfort, and aesthetic quality. Performance measures can be either objective or subjective measures. Objective measures include items such as number of sick days, accident reports, or time to complete projects, which can be gathered using archival data and existing reports. Subjective measures consist of individuals' opinions and perceptions on various topics, typically obtained through surveys or interviews with various stakeholders. POE results can lead to site and facility improvements and enhancements. They can reveal barriers, highlight specific features that impede productivity, and/or help prioritize proposed changes.

Case study 4.2 – Greiner Hall, University at Buffalo, New York

A recently completed diagnostic POE on Greiner Hall, a residential building on the University at Buffalo campus, highlights how design features can affect users' experiences (see Figure 4.2). Residence halls

4.2 Greiner Hall, University at Buffalo, New York
Photo by Douglas Levere

are home to a broad and diverse population, including students with varying needs, abilities, and interests, as well as university staff and visitors. Residence halls include spaces for sleeping, eating, studying, meeting, teaching, and gathering. The wide variety of spaces and people makes residence halls an ideal environment for implementing inclusive design features. While there have been POEs conducted on how specific features of the residence hall environments affect student satisfaction and behavior, this was the first study to examine the effect of a specific set of inclusive design strategies on a building's users.

The Center for Inclusive Design and Environmental Access conducted the POE, which the Rehabilitation Engineering Research Center on Universal Design (RERC-UD) supported, and the POE included multiple methods. First, guided tours consisted of a trained researcher who escorted 62 participants through the new residence hall and a comparison hall one at a time. The researcher asked participants to perform various tasks using the building's features throughout the tour and to rate the ease or difficulty of such tasks. The guided tour focused on usability and addressed a selected set of topics, such as entry to the building, design of public areas, finding destinations, and using features and amenities in restrooms, hallways, kitchens, lounges, stairways, elevators, and sleeping rooms. Participants consisted of paid volunteers who did not live in either building and who had a variety of physical and cognitive abilities and backgrounds.

Residents of both buildings then completed an online survey. While the guided tour focused primarily on the ease of completing tasks, the online survey asked residents to evaluate specific features in their residence hall in terms of their satisfaction, safety, and comfort. The online survey addressed (1) private areas within the halls, for example, resident's rooms or suites; (2) shared spaces, for example, lounges, bathrooms, and laundry areas; and (3) public spaces, for example, first-floor lounges and eating areas. These analogous assessments of issues or concerns – from the guided tours and the online surveys – provided researchers with the opportunity to explore new issues and to investigate suspected issues further. For example, the qualitative portion of the survey identified a problem with frequent tripping of circuit breakers, but researchers did not realize the extent of the problem until the work order analysis revealed that this issue accounted for 37% of all work orders in the new residential building.

The findings indicated that participants with disabilities benefited more greatly from inclusive features than those without disabilities, although all reported higher ratings for the newer residential hall. Participants rated the new residence hall as more usable and more satisfactory than the comparison hall. Thus, the findings confirmed the hypothesis that inclusive design provides a better user experience for all. It appears that it is possible to establish a relationship between the use of specific inclusive design strategies and user ratings.[3]

What is facility management, and what is its role in inclusive design practices?

Facility management is the process by which an organization ensures its people, buildings, systems, and services support the organization's core operations and strategic objectives. In an increasingly competitive and complex marketplace, and with rising costs, growing user expectations, and new legislation on workplace health and safety, facilities managers help provide a competitive edge. Facilities managers will downsize, outsource, or modify features and practices in order to reduce costs, increase efficiencies, and contribute to an organization's overall quality and value. The discipline requires an interdisciplinary knowledge base, including property management, space design, health and safety, emergency preparedness, environmental stewardship, human factors, technology, and maintenance. In an organization that seeks to incorporate practices that empower and support individuals with diverse needs and abilities, facilities managers perform a critical role.

Strategy 4.1 The importance of facilities managers

Facilities managers play an important but often overlooked role in the health, safety, productivity, and enjoyment of building occupants. Diligence in the cleaning and maintenance of spaces and equipment greatly improves users' performance and satisfaction. Likewise, making adjustments to how spaces are assigned and used can enhance the experiences of occupants.

Safety and security

The facilities department often manages many safety-related issues in an effort to minimize injuries, accidents, or loss of business. Security may also fall under the control of the facility management department. This includes any hardware, software, or personnel that might be necessary to protect the employees and the business. The facility management department will also oversee fire safety and security systems.

Maintenance, testing, and inspections

Maintenance, testing, and inspection schedules are required to ensure that the facility continues to operate safely and efficiently, and to maximize the life of equipment and reduce the risk of failure. The facility management department will likely have in place maintenance, inspection, and testing schedules for all fire safety equipment and systems, keeping records and certificates of compliance.

Cleaning

Cleaning responsibilities often focus on upkeep of restrooms and work areas, such as collecting and disposing of trash, replenishing supplies, and sanitizing fixtures and surfaces. Selection of maintenance times is critical. In some cases, for example, work areas, after-hours maintenance might be preferred, as it reduces interruption of workflow. In other cases, for example, busy restrooms, maintenance during business hours is desirable as a means to ensure cleanliness and reduce the likelihood of spreading disease. In both instances, facilities managers must carefully consider what supplies to use. Many cleaning chemicals can be toxic to both humans and the environment;

maintenance staff must avoid these products, particularly with the recent rise in chemical sensitivities and allergies.

Space allocation revisions

Due to changes in personnel, tasks, and projects, office and space layouts may vary. Facilities managers are responsible for planning and executing any necessary changes. The facility management department normally plans these changes using computer-aided design. In addition to meeting the needs of the business, compliance with statutory requirements related to office layouts include the minimum amount of space provided per staff member, lighting levels, signage, ventilation, and temperature control, as well as spaces for team meetings or break rooms.

Operations management

The facility management department has responsibilities for the day-to-day running of the building. In some instances, these tasks may be outsourced, while in other cases, these may be carried out directly by employed staff. When operations issues arise, for example, lights are out, the temperature is too cold, or furniture is requested, it is critical that the facility management department has a clear and expedient process for receiving and acting on notifications.

Long-term improvements

Inclusive design, at its highest level of practice, is a continual improvement process. Continual improvements, however, can be made only if there is funding allocated to that purpose. Most organizations have an annual budget for such purposes. During the design process, it is likely that some good ideas will not be possible to implement due to cost limitations. In the occupancy period, architects and other members of the design team can help develop a long-term plan, including cost estimates, to implement desirable features in the future. It is best if this list is not static. Every year, using data collected from the methods mentioned earlier, a team can review the list, identify new issues to be addressed, reassess priorities, and delete or demote items that are no longer important. If budgetary constraints do not allow improvements, the team can identify sources of funding and start a campaign to get their top priorities funded. This could include participation of constituents from the general public who use the facility and/or key change agents within the organization.

Closing the loop

For specialized architecture firms, vigorous real estate development companies, and large- and medium-scale contractors and builders, information collected during the occupancy and post-occupancy phases can inform subsequent projects. As such, this last phase in the design and construction process is not simply a last step; it is a first step. Lessons learned from past mistakes and successes can be applied to subsequent projects, particularly buildings of similar size, use, and construction. Starting a new project with a review of recently completed projects done using an inclusive design approach can further improve the likelihood of success, reduce design time, reduce construction costs, and further enhance the health, safety, performance, and satisfaction of building occupants.

Notes

1 Danford, Gary Scott, Michael Grimble, and Jordana L. Maisel. "Benchmarking the Effectiveness of Universal Designs." *The State of the Science in Universal Design: Emerging Research and Developments* 47 (2010): 65–78; and Preiser, Wolfgang F. E., and Andrea Hardy. "Historical Review of Building Performance Evaluation." *Architecture Beyond Criticism: Expert Judgment and Performance Evaluation* (2014): 147.

2 Federal Facilities Council. *Learning From Our Buildings: A State-of-the-Practice Summary of Post-Occupancy Evaluation*. Washington, DC: The National Academies Press, 2002.

3 Steinfeld, Edward, Sue Weidemann, Jonathan White, and Elyse Sigal. "Effectiveness of Design Standards in Improving Residence Hall Usability and Satisfaction." In *Proceedings From ARCC 2015: Architectural Research Centers Consortium 2015 Conference*. Chicago, IL, 2015.

Index

Page numbers in italic indicate a figure on the corresponding page.

accessibility: as architectural concept 4–5; in inclusive design 4–5, 10–11
accessibility assessments 126–127
accessibility features 64–74, 67, 69, 70, 72, 73; acoustic considerations 82–84, 84, 85; adaptable cabinetry 74–78, 76; adaptable kitchens 74–78, 75, 76; assessments 126–127; control interfaces 118–119; design factors 64–74, 67, 69, 70, 72, 73; fixtures 87–88; flooring 78–82, 81, 82; furniture 87–88; parking 64–65; ramps 68–69, 69; residential entries 72–74, 72, 73; sign systems 84–87, 86; stairs 69–71, 70; walking surfaces 65–68, 67; see also accessibility; construction, inclusive design; topographical considerations; transit integration; wayfinding
Access Living Chicago 38–39
acoustic considerations: accessibility features 82–84, 84, 85, 87; sociopetal seating 83, 84; special considerations, construction 116, 118; see also systems commissioning
adaptable cabinetry: accessibility features 74–78, 76; special

considerations, construction 115–116, 117
adaptable kitchens 74–78, 75, 76
aesthetics 5
anthropometry 3, 17–18, 18, 23–24
architect 14–15; design stage 46, 64, 83, 89, 90; responsibilities in construction 103–104; see also pre-design; project stakeholders
assembly: individual spaces 88–89; see also wayfinding
Awareness, Goals of Universal Design 3

bell curve 18; see also research, project
Body Fit: construction 98; Goals of Universal Design 3; see also human factors
budgetary considerations 36–44; continual improvement budget 42–43; cost-benefit analysis 41–42; inclusive design as a value proposition 36–38; life cycle costing 40–41; operating budget 39–40
building servicer 16; see also pre-design; project stakeholders
building tradespeople 105

case studies: Access Living Chicago 38–39; big-box stores 62; cabinet design 77–78; detailing cabinet assemblies 115; glass stairs *81, 82*; interactive wayfinding 86, *86–87*; post-occupancy evaluation 130–133, *131*; retrofitting lighting fixtures 129; SmartCode 25–27; thermal comfort scenario 118–119; thresholds 80; water fountains 98–100, *99*

circulation (movement) system 52–58; edges 56; markers 55, *55–56*; nodes 56; paths 53–54, *54*; zones 57–58; *see also* transit integration

classrooms: individual spaces 89–90; *see also* acoustic considerations; furniture; lighting

cleaning *see* facility manager

clients 16; *see also* pre-design; project stakeholders

CM *see* construction manager

Comfort, Goals of Universal Design 3

commercial 90–91

communication, quality control 122–124

complete streets 29–31; *see also* pre-design; site selection

connectivity of transportation 27–31, *29*; *see also* pre-design; site selection

construction, inclusive design: acoustic considerations 116, 118; adaptable cabinetry 115–116, *117*; architect 103–104; Body Fit 98; building tradespeople 105; construction manager 104–105; contractors 105; control interfaces 118–119; inclusive *versus* conventional 97–102, *99, 101*; manufacturer's representative 106; owner's representative 103–104; parking 107–108; quality control 100–102, *101*, 120–124; ramps 108–110; residential entries 111–115, *113, 114*; responsible parties 103–106; sign systems 119–120; specialized

training 106–107; stairs 110–111; walking surfaces 108–110; *see also* accessibility features; special considerations, construction

construction manager 104–105

continual improvement budget 42–43; *see also* pre-design

contractors 15, 105; *see also* pre-design; project stakeholders

control interfaces 118–119; *see also* systems commissioning

cost-benefit analysis 41–42; *see also* value proposition

CS *see* complete streets

Cultural Appropriateness, Goals of Universal Design 3

design factors 46–95; accessibility features 64–74, *67, 69, 70, 72, 73*; environmental controls 58–64, *59, 60, 63*; HVAC systems 63–64; individual spaces 88–95; lighting 59–63, *59, 60, 63*; site design 47–52, *50, 51*; wayfinding 49, 52–58

developers 14; *see also* pre-design; project stakeholders

dimensional tolerances 120–122

dwelling spaces 91–94, *93*; *see also* accessibility; acoustic considerations; HVAC systems; lighting

economic factors, inclusive design 8–10

edges 56

end user 16–17, 33–35; *see also* pre-design; project stakeholders

environmental controls 58–64, *59, 60, 63*; lighting 59–63, *59, 60, 63*

environmental factors 50–51

facility manager 15–16, 133–135; *see also* pre-design; project stakeholders financiers 14; *see also* pre-design; project stakeholders

fixtures: accessibility features 87–88; lighting 59–63; *see also* quality control

flexhousing 94

flooring 78–82, *81, 82*; *see also* quality control

focus groups 20; *see also* pre-design; research, project

furniture 87–88; *see also* quality control

getting started, inclusive design 13–19, 31–36

goals: client 32–33; project 31–32; *see also* getting started; pre-design

Goals of Universal Design: Awareness 3; Body Fit 3, 98; Comfort 3; Cultural Appropriateness 3; Personalization 3; Social Integration 3; Understanding 3; Wellness 3; *see also* anthropometry

grading 49–50, *50*

green building *see* sustainability

human diversity 2, 46

human factors, inclusive design 6–7

HVAC systems 63–64

IKEA, 115

inclusive design 36–38; accessibility in 4–5, 10–11; aesthetics 5; case studies 25–27, 38–39; construction 97–124, *99, 101, 113, 114, 117*; decision-making process in 11; definition 2–4; design factors 46–95; economic factors 8–10; human factors 6–7; innovation in 10–11; occupancy *128, 131,* 145–154; other architectural concepts 4–5; pre-design 13–44; social factors 7–8; as value proposition 36–38; *see also* Seven Principles of Universal Design

inclusive programming 31–36; end user 16–17, 33–35; spatial hierarchy 35–36

individual spaces: assembly spaces 88–89; classrooms 89–90; commercial spaces 90–91; design factors 88–95; dwelling spaces 90–91, *91–94, 93*; lavatories 94–95; performance spaces 88–89; *see also* accessibility; acoustic considerations; HVAC systems; lighting

innovation, inclusive design 10–11

innovative solutions for Universal Design website 106

interviews 21; *see also* pre-design; research, project

lavatories 94–95; *see also* accessibility; lighting; wayfinding

life cycle costing 40–41; *see also* pre-design

Lifetime Homes 29

lighting 59–63, *59, 60, 63*; electric 59–62, *59, 60*; natural 60, 62–63, *63*; retrofitting lighting fixtures case study 129; side 62–63, *63*; top 62–63, *63*; *see also* quality control; systems commissioning

maintenance, building *see* facility manager

manufacturer's representative 106

markers 55, 55–56

motivational interviewing 22; *see also* pre-design; research, project

neighborhood context *30, 31*; *see also* pre-design; site selection

nodes 56

observations 20; *see also* pre-design; research, project

occupancy: accessibility assessments 126–127; facility manager 133–135; inclusive design *128*, *131*, 145–154; post-occupancy evaluation 130–133, *131*; shakedown 125–129

occupancy demands 34–35

operating budget 39–40; *see also* pre-design

operations manager *see* facility manager

owner's representative 103–104

parking: accessibility features 64–65; special considerations, construction 107–108; *see also* quality control

paths 53–54, *54*

performance: individual spaces 88–89; *see also* acoustic considerations; HVAC systems; lighting

Personalization, Goals of Universal Design 3

POE *see* post-occupancy evaluation

post-occupancy evaluation 130–133, *131*

precedent studies 18–19; *see also* pre-design; research, project

pre-design 13–44; budgetary considerations 36–44; getting started 13–19, 31–36; project stakeholders 13–17; research, project 17–24; site selection 24–31

project goals 31–32

project stakeholders 13–17

quality control: communication 122–124; construction, inclusive design 100–102, *101*, 120–124

ramps: accessibility features 68–69, *69*; special considerations, construction 108–110; *see also* quality control

reflexivity 22; *see also* pre-design; research, project

research, foundational 22–23; *see also* pre-design; research, project

research, project 17–24

research, qualitative 22; *see also* research, project

research, targeted 22–23; *see also* pre-design; research, project

residential entries: accessibility features 72–74, *72, 73*; special considerations, construction 111–115, *113, 114*; *see also* quality control

right-of-way designs 29–31

ROW *see* right-of-way designs

saturation 22

Seven Principles of Universal Design 3

sign systems 84–87, *86*; special considerations, construction 119–120; *see also* quality control

site design 47–52, *50, 51*; environmental factors 50–51; grading 49–50, *50*; topographical considerations 47–50; transit integration *51*, 51–52; water management 47–48; *see also* design factors; site selection

site selection 24–31; *see also* site design

SmartCode 25–27; *see also* pre-design; zoning

social diversity 2, 34–35

social factors, inclusive design 7–8

Social Integration, Goals of Universal Design 3

sociopetal seating 83, *84*, 87

spatial considerations 35–36, 52–58

special considerations, construction: acoustic considerations 116, 118; adaptable cabinetry 115–116; major issues 120; residential entries 111–115, *113, 114*; sign systems 119–120; stairs 110–111; walking surfaces 108–110

specialized training: construction, inclusive design 106–107;

innovative solutions for Universal Design website 106

stairs: accessibility features 69–71, 70; special considerations, construction 110–111; *see also* quality control

strategy synopses: complementary features 71; gathering useful information 19; getting started 13; HVAC systems 64; the importance of facilities managers 134; leveraging the knowledge of trade workers 105; lighting 60; priority parking 65; resolving unforeseen challenges 102

surveys 20–21; *see also* pre-design; research, project

sustainability, as architectural concept 4

systems commissioning 127–129

topographical considerations 47–50, 50

transect zones 25–27; T1 Natural 25; T2 Rural 25; T3 Suburban 25–26; T4 General Urban 26; T5 Urban Center 27; T6 Urban Core 27; *see also* pre-design; zoning

transit integration: right-of-way designs 29–31; site design 51, 51–52

transportation considerations 27–31; *see also* pre-design; site selection

triangulation 22

T zone *see* transect zones

Understanding, Goals of Universal Design 3

universal design 3, 98, 103–106; *see also* anthropometry; inclusive design

user input 19; *see also* pre-design; research, project

user interface *see* control interfaces

validation 22

value proposition 36–38; *see also* budgetary considerations

walking surfaces 65–68, 67; accessibility features 65–68, 67; special considerations, construction 108–110; *see also* quality control

water management 47–48

wayfinding 49, 52–58; circulation (movement) system 52–58; definition 52; edges 56; interactive maps 86, 86–87; markers 55, 55–56; nodes 56; paths 53–54, 54; sign systems 84–87, 86; spatial considerations 52–58; zones 57–58; *see also* transit integration

Wellness, Goals of Universal Design 3

zones 57–58

zoning 24–27; Euclidean 24; form-based 25; incentive-based 25; performance-based 24; *see also* pre-design; site selection